Creating a Profitable Garden Center

Greg Moore

Creating a Profitable Garden Center
Copyright © 2025
By Greg Moore

Chapters of Life
Toledo, Washington
www.chaptersoflife.com

ISBN 978-0-9768272-6-9 print

Library of Congress Control Number:

Cover design by Kathy Campbell
Dreamstime (back) and iStock (front) Credit: KeithBishop Stock photo ID:1402494203

Subjects: Gardening / Flowers / Nursery / Business / Entrepreneur / Garden Center / Pacific Northwest

It's been said that
an hour in the garden
puts life's problems
into perspective.
Your job is to get them there.

Contents

Preface

How did this book come into being? That's easy. I've spent over forty years in the retail garden center business. With the knowledge I've gained, I've mapped out a plan for your success and am excited to share it with you. One thing about this business is that you're constantly learning. This has been a good fit for me; I love to learn. This business makes you hungry to learn more. You become a teacher. A teacher to your staff. A teacher to your customers. And you yourself are constantly learning. This is a business that allows you to use your head and your hands. And if that's not enough, you work outside most of the time. This is undeniably a fantastic business to be in. You meet lots of great people; you enrich people's lives every day, and in return, they enrich yours. With all the great things about this business, I feel I've never worked a day in my life. I feel the need to share some of the wisdom—wisdom I've gained through the years—about running a garden center successfully. There are lots of tricks to being successful with growing living things, working with the public, and fostering good staff. I hope this book is helpful.

Introduction

This is a simple-to-understand how-to guide for ownership or management of a garden center. The information in this book has been gathered over nearly half a century in the garden center business. The information herein covers experiences in the many aspects of the business. This information will be helpful in understanding what it takes to be a successful garden center owner or manager. There are many phases to this operation. This book will cover most of them. Use this guide to understand what it takes to develop a nursery from the ground up. It will also inform you about the many ways of keeping your garden center running smoothly and efficiently. This should be a good learning manual for the beginner or for the seasoned nursery professional. I'm sure you'll find useful information to make your job easier. Now, let's go sell some plants!

Acknowledgments

I would like to thank John Stanley and Ian Baldwin for their tireless efforts in supporting and promoting this great industry for so many years. You both have helpled guide and teach generations of nursery folks. And we appreciate it. Louis Berninger, whose book Profitable Garden Center Management was my first college textbook in 1980. This set me on my path to begin understanding this business. Kings and Pricketts Nurseries of Santa Rosa, California, were my introduction to the garden center world as a child in the early 1960s. A real wonderland for a kid to explore. Though much has changed, both nurseries are still going strong today. Thanks for keeping a child's dream alive.

A huge heartfelt acknowledgment goes to my mentor, the late Paul Ricketts. His nursery, Paul's Garden Shop, got me started professionally in this fabulous business as a kid of twenty who wanted to learn. Without his support, knowledge, and patience, I wouldn't be in this position today. He taught me the love of the business. Because of him, I changed my college direction from an English degree to horticulture and business majors. I use his wisdom often and am forever thankful for his guidance.

And finally, a big thank you to the folks at Voluntary Purchasing Group for helping my Garden Center thrive, namely my VPG sales rep Mark Taylor for all his support. Without his encouragement, this book wouldn't have come to fruition.

Creating a Profitable Garden Center

Getting Started

IN THE BEGINNING you really need to know what you're getting into. The hours are long, and the knowledge needed is immense. The industry is vast, complex, challenging, and exciting. And at the same time, it is very stressful. Your business is "seasonal" and all seasonal businesses share this: a lot of business (and hopefully money) all at once, then it stops. The trick is learning how to work with this and not spending it all during the off season.

The nursery business is constantly changing. To be successful you will need to make changes too. You'll need to diversify your inventory based on market needs and trends. Don't jump in too fast. Allow your business to settle in, then add new products as you go. You can overspend quickly if you're not careful. Here are the basics for getting started in your new venture:

Securing Legal Help

Before getting started, you'll have to obtain some help behind the scenes. An attorney will help with your legal matters. They will be the first person you'll need to contact before setting out. They will draw up the necessary contracts you'll need to form your business. They will also be there to advise you as you go along. Your attorney is there to represent you, and the business, should legal matters arise. This is a must-have for your business. When you find an attorney that meets your business needs, keep them. They will grow with you and understand your business as it grows.

Next in line is your accountant. Again a must-have for your business. You will count on them more than you may realize. They're not just the ones to prepare your tax forms at the end of the year. They are there to advise and represent you and the business all year long. You'll be surprised how often you find yourself reaching out to them. Tax issues and what you can write off are only a few issues they will help you with. Again, the advice here is that when you find an accountant you're comfortable with, keep them. They too will grow with your business, and they'll understand it more as you go along.

The bookkeeping aspect of your business is vital. You have to keep good books for your company. To do this, you'll need a bookkeeper who understands your business. This may be someone in-house or hired out. Your bookkeeper, like your attorney and accountant, is a big part of what happens behind the scenes. Again, when you find a good one, keep them.

Keep in mind that these three people cost money. This is something you need to be aware of. Their services don't come cheap. Nonetheless they are vital to your business. Be prepared to have money allotted for their services. Also, be prepared to file two sets of tax returns each year. One for you, one for the business.

Making a Solid Plan

With any business, you must have a plan before you start. The basic plan is to develop, hire, and sell. Here is what you need first:

- nursery industry knowledge
- general business knowledge
- general knowledge of the plants
- chemical and hard goods knowledge
- plant troubleshooting
- vendors
- location
- a bank loan
- contractor

- ✔ permits
- ✔ inventory
- ✔ supplies
- ✔ staff
- ✔ budgeting plan

Understanding the Seasons

It is of utmost importance that you understand the seasons and how they work. The winter is for preparing for the spring (busy) season. This is the time to get the ordering done, the crew taught, and the projects completed. The twelve golden weeks will follow. During April, May, and June, you will make the money for the entire year. If you have the right weather and inventory, this period may begin sooner and go into the summer. With that said, you will have business throughout the year; however, your main focus, and that of your customers, is spring. It is during this period that you need to push your products in order to maximize sales. This includes a big focus on tie-in sales. This is your big, and only, chance to put money in the bank. You don't get a second chance. You'll need to have current and fresh inventory at all times. You should prepare to have bedding trucks delivering weekly or more often. (More on this later.) You'll need to be aware of the weather. Bad weather can slow your sales. You must have good control of your payroll. You need adequate staff; keep a tight watch on this. Too many employees? Send some home. It's your money; be in control of it. This is also the time of the year to be putting money aside for winter. As the summer comes, your staff should be in maintenance mode. A lot of time is spent on the hose, grooming, and sales. The fall months provide the same responsibilities and business—with less inventory, of course. Payroll should be adjusted to accommodate your sales.

Scoping the Competition

It's important to know what, and who, you're up against. You'll need to have a very close look at this. Since your inventories will be similar, care needs to be made to compare with what your competitor is doing. Here is what to consider:

- ✔ Where are your competitors located?
- ✔ What is their main sales focus?
- ✔ What about pricing?
- ✔ What is the quality of their inventory?
- ✔ What is the overall condition of the store?
- ✔ Do they have knowledgeable staff?
- ✔ How good is their curb appeal?
- ✔ How established are they in the community?
- ✔ Do you want to (and can you) compete with them?

Making Money

When all your ducks are in a row, you're ready to start making money. As long as you have good inventory, staff, etc., you're ready. Remember, the key to making money lies in your purchasing. You always have to buy smart to sell smart; that's the rule. (More on this later.) That said, don't expect big gains the first year you are in business. Your business will be in its developing phase. Word has to spread throughout your community. Your advertising needs to work. Your business has to create name recognition. And most importantly, you have to establish a customer base. Finding and supporting your niche will take time by itself. Don't overbuy. This is learned over time. The last thing your nursery needs is to have unselling inventory tying up your much needed money. Diversifying your inventory takes time too. Plan ahead. Start with your green goods and basic tie-ins, fertilizers, chemicals, potting soils, etc., and go from there. Most new businesses will fail in the first five years. Be smart with your money. Don't watch it go away.

Some Added Notes

- ✔ Be prepared to work long hours.
- ✔ Never stop learning your craft.
- ✔ Winters can be financially challenging.
- ✔ Monitor the payroll closely.
- ✔ Keep enthusiastic staff.
- ✔ Your image will define your success.

- ✔ Gardening dollars are leisure dollars.
- ✔ Be 100 percent ready for the twelve golden weeks.
- ✔ If it were easy to run a garden center, everyone would.

Your Job

YOU ALONE CREATE YOUR BUSINESS IMAGE. You are responsible for teaching your staff about how you want the store to be viewed. You're in charge of your inventory, pricing, staff issues, customer service, accounting, and so much more. You are, or will become, the ultimate problem solver. You will solve many problems every day. Every time you turn the key in the door, it's showtime. But in reality, so much more happens before, and after, the door is closed. You live and breathe this business you've created. It consumes you; it has to. It's your money and your dream; it's your life.

Remember this: Your job adds smiles to people's faces. I was told once, "We don't sell plants, we sell smiles." Your customers are trying to avoid the stresses in life by visiting your store. You need to always remember this. You need to keep your nursery interesting and exciting. Your inventory focus should be different than that of your competitors. You'll always need to keep your attention and focus on these four words: quality, service, selection, and value. Never let any of these slip. Create and protect a squeaky clean image. This is important because good news in your community travels fast, bad news even faster.

About You

You must be prepared to oversee everything about your store. You need to be organized, self-motivated, and aware of all departments. You must have your finger on the pulse of your business at all times. Here are some of the prerequisites:

- ✔ Do you have business sense?
- ✔ Do you have mental and physical stamina?
- ✔ Have you worked in a garden center before?
- ✔ Are you a good leader?
- ✔ Can you delegate and organize?
- ✔ Will the public feel you know your stuff, and do you?
- ✔ Are you able to maximize your time by working long hours?
- ✔ Will you be able to let the small stuff go?

These are some tools you must possess in order to successfully run a garden center. If you're weak on any of these points, you'll need to work on them or find another business to get into.

What You Gotta Do

Teach your crew and your customers with a good dose of common sense. Your vision and this business may be new to your crew. Teach in ways they'll understand. Talk slowly and be a good listener. Never assume anything. The trick is to keep gardening simple, basic, and understandable for both your staff and your customers. Communication is key. Be sure everyone understands what you're trying to convey. The knowledge of your business is foreign to many people you'll be exposed to. Be thorough and complete while teaching both your crew and your customers. Excite your team and keep them motivated. Lead by example. Expect the best. Be fair. Never assume your staff will understand your dream. You'll have to teach that. Take the time to teach your team why we do things the way we do, not just how. This will help with better understanding. Enforce that "there's never nothing to do." The slow times are spent being productive. Cleaning, ordering, repotting, bench repairing, and signing are just a few of the tasks that need undertaking. Always take advantage of the slow times to the fullest. You don't ever get this time back.

Knowledge

You must select premier growers and hard goods suppliers for your garden center. Without exceptional products, you're no different than any of your competitors. Always have great quality, great selection, and fair pricing for your customers.

Study problem solving. Your customers will expect you to have the answers they need. After all, you are the gardening expert.

You are constantly learning and teaching. This is what you can expect. You'll learn a lot from your customers too. The public has a wealth of knowledge to tap into. You will always, or should always, be adding to your plant and hard goods knowledge. Knowing when to purchase inventory is a lesson in itself. This comes in time. Some of your inventory will need to be ordered six to eight months in advance. You can't expect to go into the spring ordering just what you need. It doesn't work that way.

Employee Handbooks

You should have three employee handbooks for your staff. One handbook should explain the legal parts of the business that pertains to them. The next handbook should spell out their job description. This way your crew will know what's expected of them, and what to expect. This should be presented when they are hired. The third handbook should explain (in a very basic way) the general aspects of the nursery for your new staff members. Outlines for these three handbooks are located in the Your Staff chapter. It's up to you to create, enforce, and teach from these handbooks.

The Unexpected

Preparing for the unexpected is something you'll have to do. If you're prepared, there's no problem. If you're not, it could be catastrophic. Say, for instance, you're making it through your first year just fine. Things are tight, but okay. All of a sudden, the transmission goes out on the delivery truck. Enter the unexpected. Or a customer falls in the yard; are you covered? There are many unexpected things that can happen in your business. Here's a short list to keep in mind:

- inventory and equipment break
- credit card processing fees

- crew issues
- taxes, the unexpected bill you'll always owe
- customer problems
- expensive utilities
- COD accounts from vendors you can't pay
- limited inventory space for product
- not enough money to cover payroll

Some Additional Notes

- Always think and plan ahead, maybe the night before.
- Keep a tight control on your spending. Make money, don't watch it go away.
- Prepare for long winters.
- Keep revisiting your one- and five-year plans.
- Twenty percent of today's workforce is working from home. Your job is to get them into your nursery.
- Your ultimate goal is to satisfy customers.
- Change in your business is everything. Always keep it current and exciting.
- Pay close attention to your profit and loss statement. Review this monthly.
- Visit other nurseries at least once a year.
- Build and keep your image.
- Attend seminars a few times each year.
- Control payroll.
- You are in control.
- Now the job begins.

Your To-Do List

You've got so many things to be responsible for. That goes without saying. Without being organized, you're in trouble. I've always felt that organization is the key to success. You're going to need a to-do list for yourself. This will help with your ordering, staff notes, projects, and all the other things that only you can do. I've used a to-do list for years. Without it I'd be lost. You have to stay focused and ahead of the game. It often seems that something of real importance comes to mind and is forgotten quickly by other interferences. This "something" may become a problem if it's not written down. With so much going on all the time (especially during spring), and so much at stake, you have to stay on top of everything. Your list may also include things you feel only you are capable of doing, or things that would simply take too long to explain to a staff member.

Selecting a Banker

WHEN YOU FIND A GOOD BANKER, keep them. You need to consider your banker a business partner. They will know everything in the financial part of your business. You will have to be open and honest with them about your goals, plans, and financial strategy. You need to convince your banker both verbally and on paper that you have the means to be successful. Many businesses fail in the first three to five years. Your banker knows this and wants to ensure loaning money to you is a good and sound idea.

An additional note: It's a really good idea to get to know your banker. After all, they're really like a business partner to you. Show an interest in their life. They will in yours. This relationship should last for the duration of your business. Do lunch from time to time. Drop in to just say hello once in a while. A quick, nonformal, meeting will show your interest in them as a person. This is a small way of showing your appreciation to them for all they have done, and will continue to do, for you and your company. These small gestures will pay dividends to you. If your banker changes banks, change banks with them. This shows your continued support and trust in them. And by all means, keep your bank accounts with their bank.

Your Business Plan

✔ Do you have the knowledge to run this venture?

- ✔ How will you pay off the loan?
- ✔ What inventory will set you apart from your competitor?
- ✔ How will you market your store?
- ✔ How will you target your audience?
- ✔ How will you be successful?

You will need to be complete but easy to understand in your approach with your banker. Try not to confuse your banker with nursery language. They might not understand your plant world. They are more concerned with the money part of the business anyway.

What the Bank Needs

- ✔ a strong mission statement
- ✔ a resume showing your background
- ✔ a personal financial statement
- ✔ one-year and five-year marketing and sales plans
- ✔ a completed loan application
- ✔ your start-up needs (non-inventory)
- ✔ your salable inventory

This is just a short list of what is needed to secure a Small Business Administration (SBA) loan. Your banker will certainly need more information. Be sure to allow six to eight months for your paperwork to be processed. Business loans take time. Don't wait till the last minute. And by all means, come to the bank as prepared as possible. It's also a good idea to have your certified public accountant (CPA) look over your paperwork before submitting it. They will find things you may have missed.

The SBA Loan

The Small Business Administration loan is the easiest, and most reliable, loan to get for your business. The bank will do much of the paperwork for you. Again, this will take time to process. You can get a low-interest loan to be paid over a decided-upon period of time. The SBA wants to promote small businesses. They are easy to work with and are the most effective way to finance your business venture. It doesn't hurt to ask family members for a small loan to show as money in your bank account. This looks good on your application and is returned as soon as your loan is approved.

How much money should you ask for? This can be tricky. You want to look at your costs very carefully. Will the figures you counted on be the same in the time period it takes for loan approval? This would include your building costs, labor, inventory, and about anything else you can think of. Speaking of that, you'll want to add an additional twenty percent to your loan for the unexpected. Even though you have been complete with this, there will always be unexpected costs. Be fair to yourself. Don't cut yourself short. If you fall short, you'll have to come up with the rest on your own.

The Line of Credit

An operating line of credit (LOC) may be useful for your business. The line of credit will help you get through the slow seasons, and, if necessary, purchase inventory for the next busy season. Some feel this LOC is an essential part of running a garden center. It's good to know there's money available when you need it. The line is renewed each year. This means it needs to be paid off before it's renewed. Your inventory is used as collateral. It's relatively easy to establish. Your banker will review your balance sheet to determine the amount of your loan based on your amount of existing inventory. Again, it's a good idea to get the paperwork going well before you'll need the money. Your banker does all the paperwork for you, so it's relatively easy. But remember, you will have to pay it back every year. I would recommend using July as a beginning and maturing date for your LOC loan. This way you will have the busy spring months to pay the loan off well ahead of when it's due.

Selecting Your Location

WHERE YOU ARE PLANNING to put your garden center can make or break you. It's that simple. You have to do your homework and your legwork before you decide. This is one of the biggest decisions in life you have to make. Will your business be successful?

~ The Community

Is this an established community? Are there other garden centers there? Are they close to the area you would like to put your shop? If so, what's their main focus? Are they successful? How long have these other businesses been in existence?

~ Population

How many people live in this area? What's the average age? Your target audience is between thirty- to sixty-year-olds. A demographic study of the area will tell you this. How often people move into, and out of, your potential market is important too.

~ Income

The median income of your customer base is of huge importance. Do they have enough extra income for leisure purchases such as yours? Low-income areas won't be able to support you. On the reverse side, high-income areas may have little or no interest in you either. This is an important consideration.

~ Local Economy

How strong is the local economy in your potential market? Have businesses been established in this area a long time? How often do new businesses close their doors? A strong and thriving economy is what you're looking for. Without a good local economy, you will most likely struggle.

~ Newly Developing Areas

Will you plan to set up shop in a newly developing market? Are these mainly single-family homes? Is this area mostly town houses, condos, and apartments? Your ideal setting would be near a newly developing town with single-family homes. These new homeowners are going to need your business. This is really an ideal setting.

~ Shopping Center

Have you considered setting up your garden center in, or near, a shopping center? This can go a couple of ways. If your customers are shopping door-to-door on foot they will find you. However, they may be limited in what they buy due to having to carry their purchases. If you plan to sell smaller items, this may work. If you're planning on being a full-service store (trees, shrubs, etc.), this will be very limiting. If your potential customer's vehicle is close, this could change for the better. If you are considering your location in the parking lot of a shopping center, people may not see you. It's true; whether you're surrounded by cars or just seem out of place, you just seem to be invisible to customers. I've seen many of these shops fail.

Do your homework before you select your spot, and certainly before you visit your banker. These are all important factors to consider when selecting your perfect spot. Ask yourself this: Can I picture myself, my shop, crew, and customers here? It should feel good.

Buying an Established Nursery

~ Location

Is the location good for what you're planning or has it worn away through the years others have owned it? Has the neighborhood developed around the garden center, seemingly smothering the store? Has the store lost its charm, and if it has, can you bring it back? What would it take, and are you willing to take that gamble? Has the real estate in the area gotten to the point where the land is too valuable to support a nursery?

~ Condition

Are the buildings in good repair and are the utilities still in working order? How are the store displays? How is the greenhouse? The benches, covered areas, and pathways? Are you willing to put out the money and effort to make it yours?

~ Current Inventory

How much inventory is there? What shape is it in? Are the plants overgrown, underfed, and struggling? Are your dry goods and chemicals outdated with faded labels? Can much, or any, of this be salvaged? At what cost or effort on your part is it worth salvaging? Putting a value on all of the current inventory is hard. The current owner will always feel the inventory is worth more than it realistically is. A fair market value may be hard to agree on. For the most part the inventory is only worth its wholesale price or less. If you're considering the location but can't agree on a fair price for the inventory, you may have the current owner liquidate with a sale before you take over. This could have bad aftereffects, however. Customers will know that the store is going out of business and forget, or not be aware, that your new store will be coming soon.

~ Image

What type of image does the store have? Did the previous owner treat customers fairly? If not, that may reflect on you. A new store with a questionable image will be hard to overcome with previous customers. You'll have to begin advertising right away to let the public know about you and what you sell. With this advertising campaign, you'll certainly need to talk about change and what makes your store better than ever.

~ Goodwill

Goodwill is always the hardest point to agree on when negotiating the deal. The current owner will undoubtedly believe that during the time they owned the store, they built a strong following with a lot of goodwill attached. This is always one of the sensitive areas for two businesspeople to agree on. Somehow this needs to be addressed before a deal can be made. The current owner usually has to back down some as far as goodwill is concerned.

~ Other Concerns

Is the location visible? What about traffic flow? Is there easy access from the street? What about adequate parking? What about good access for deliveries? Is the available water able to meet your needs? Is there room to expand? These are all necessary issues to be addressed whether you plan on purchasing an existing business or start elsewhere.

From the Ground Up

Your view from the street is of utmost importance. Untidy, ungroomed color displays can have a poor effect. Customers may simply pass you by, assuming the rest of your place has similar unkept plants. Color displays, of course, are put into place once your location has been secured but are nonetheless an important part of making the public aware of you.

~ Permits

Before you select and purchase the lot of your choice, you'll need to research permits. The city or county may not permit you to create your garden center in your chosen spot. You can find this out from the local building and planning department or the county office. You have to do this first. Many businesses have purchased property only to find they can't do what they wanted to do, and they have to sell the property. This is a life lesson you don't want. You'll also have to contact your local fire department before building. They may require a fire hydrant installed to service your building in the event of a fire. You may need to have a traffic study done as well. This is to see how your business may impact local traffic. You may also need to have a sidewalk installed in front of your store. All these factors are involved in the permitting process to allow your store to be created to begin with. These things all happened to me when I developed my garden center. These can be unexpected, expensive costs to be figured into your loan amount.

~ The Street Sign

Your street sign may well be your most important part of the start-up process. This too will need a permit. Your sign lets the public know where you are. They can be simple or complex. Don't crowd your sign. Keep it simple with your name only. Drivers won't be able to read much more than your name while passing your store. Raise it high enough to be noticed. Again, check with local city and county officials first. There are usually height restrictions.

~ Parking

Your customers will need plenty of parking spaces during the spring rush. Be sure your store can accommodate this. Without sufficient places to park, you may lose customers. It's also a good idea to have some overflow parking for the busy season. This may be as simple as sharing your neighbor's parking lot. Sometimes it even works out that your neighbor's store may be closed on the weekends. That's when you can really use these extra parking spaces. It's always a good idea to be friendly with your neighbors anyway. A little friendliness goes a long way when you're hoping for some extra seasonal parking. However, you don't want your overflow to impact their business at any cost. Be smart about it.

~ Fencing

Is your potential garden center already fenced? If so, is the fence in good shape or does it need some work? Fencing is an essential part of your establishment. If there is no fence, you'll have to erect one. This is yet another one of the many somewhat hidden charges you may not have thought about. It will need a permit too. Again, more money. And again, this cost will need to be planned on and added into your original bank loan.

~ Additional Considerations

1. Will your shop be on a main road and in the public eye? It should be. Otherwise, you can plan on more advertising to let your customers know where you are.

2. Is your selected spot level with good drainage? This will need to be dealt with before anything happens. This may be a considerable cost. You will need to get bids (usually three) for this and add it to the amount needed for your bank loan.

3. Will the lot size be large enough to accommodate your nursery building, or buildings? Is there ample space for your shade area? Is there enough room for your can yard? These are all important questions to ask yourself.

4. Gravel or asphalt surfaces can be a concern for you. Many nurseries use gravel in their can yard. It's one of the few businesses that can use gravel as their surface. Gravel has its benefits. It's inexpensive compared to asphalt and it drains your water away quickly. The other benefit of gravel is that you won't have a wastewater reclamation fee in areas that have a fee for that. The downside of gravel is that it may be hard for some of your customers to walk on. It's hard for some carts with small tires to be able to navigate over as well. Asphalt or concrete are expensive. Both, however, won't need to be replaced as quickly as gravel. It's better if you find a lot that already has a base with asphalt or gravel so you can save on the expense.

5. Prime locations, high rents. It's the old "you get what you pay for" line. You may want to position your garden center on a busy street in the middle of town. However, the high rent will make it impossible for your type of business to afford it. On the flipside, inexpensive rent areas may not be desirable either. It's best to find an area with middle-of-the-road rent in order to not feel pinched. The same holds true in regard to land values if you're planning to purchase the lot and build from the ground up. Be careful and choose wisely.

Start-Up Costs

BESIDES DECIDING TO GO INTO BUSINESS, the most important consideration will be how much money you'll need. This may end up being a large sum. Whatever you do, make sure you've thought of everything before going to the bank for your loan. Don't cut corners by underestimating your costs. The likelihood is that they'll be more. After you've checked and checked again just how much it will take, add twenty percent for unforeseen costs. You can expect the unexpected. Don't cut yourself short. The following list may help you prepare.

The Property

- ✔ own
- ✔ rent
- ✔ or lease

Development Costs

- ✔ the nursery building
- ✔ outbuildings, greenhouses
- ✔ covered area for bedding

- benches
- irrigation
- shade area
- pathways
- water
- backflow preventers
- fire hydrant
- parking lot paving
- fencing
- carts, hoses, misc. outdoor supplies
- security cameras
- indoor displays, counters, etc.
- office area computers, copier, desks, etc.
- point-of-sale (POS) area registers and visa machines
- phone lines, internet service, and misc. equipment
- carryout boxes
- initial inventory
- permits
- bookkeeper
- CPA
- attorney
- extra twenty percent for misc.

As you can see there's a lot more than you may have originally thought. This doesn't include staff or your wages. If possible, try to run tight on payroll for your first year or so. Plan to work extra hours to help keep this down. You can always add extra help when you need it. This is the best plan anyway. Payroll is the one thing you have control of.

The Nursery Layout

YOUR GARDEN CENTER SHOULD BE INVITING and comfortable. Your store needs to have a traffic flow that allows your customers to explore and see everything you have. The aisles should be easy to walk through with a cart without bumping into others. Paths should be somewhat intimate as well, with lots to discover on the way. Keep in mind that your traffic flow is the only way your customers will see it all. It's a good idea to design your store and yard on paper first. Keep your paths in accordance with the Americans with Disabilities Act (ADA).

Inside the Shop

Above all, your store needs to be clean. Since you sell dirt, this is an ongoing process. Your aisles should be free of merchandise at all times. You're in retail, so the store needs to be accessible and inviting. The aisles need to be ADA friendly as well. This means your aisles need to be thirty-six inches wide. Also, if your aisles are more than 200 feet long, you must have 60 inches of clearance for passing other shoppers. Customers, without a doubt, will bring carts into your store. You want them to feel comfortable doing so. Sometimes you will have several carts in the building at the same time. This, of course, is a common occurrence during the spring rush. Be ready for this before it happens. Your endcap displays of promotional, or impulse, items should feature only one item for maximum sales effect. The displays should always be well signed. The first endcap display your customers will see is the display immediately inside your front door. This one has the most impact of any displays in your store. This endcap or island display needs to be well thought-out. Plan your promotions in this spot carefully. Again, good signing is essential here. As a footnote, this display should be no closer than six to eight feet from your front door. Customers like to mingle in this area, so give them space.

Soft background music is a good idea. Don't use the radio for this. It tends to distract your customers' thinking process. Soft jazz usually works well as a format. Never play your music loud. This is a distraction. Another rule is to always have yourself, or management, be responsible for the style of music and the volume. Your staff may have other ideas that may not be of suitable taste for your store's image.

Providing coffee for your customers is a good idea. It is especially welcomed in the cold regions of the North. You will find that the locals will tend to stay, and hopefully shop, longer if you have coffee on. Customers will gather around the coffee pot for some small talk too (usually about plants).

You may also consider a sitting area. This lets folks take a break while their other half is shopping. Providing some cookies or the like from time to time isn't a bad idea either. Your customers will like this addition to your place. Many will grow to expect it too. This is just another way to show your customers you appreciate them and value their business. It may be a small gesture that sets you aside from your competition. A small business trick.

Scented candles and the like may seem like a good idea; however, some of your customers may not like the scent, or be allergic to the particular scent you've chosen. It may seem pleasant to you but may not be for everybody. How many times have you walked into a store only to be overwhelmed by a scent they're using? If you're going to sell candles, don't light them. This is a safety move as well. Be careful with all air piercing fragrances.

The Checkout Counter

This may seem like an easy placement to you. There are some things to keep in mind, though. Your placement should be somewhere close to the front door.

It should stand out and be clearly marked. You may need several for your operation. The counter should be no higher than thirty inches. Your customers will appreciate this height. Plants can be heavy from the cart. The counter should be long enough to handle quite a few plants. I would suggest a minimum of six feet in length. This too will accommodate quite a few plants.

Keep your counters clear! I can't overstate this enough. Your counter should only be for your customers' purchases. Too often I've seen super crowded counters. This makes finding room for plants and other items rather challenging. Your register, visa machine, and maybe your newsletter is all that should be on your counter. Prevent staff from keeping drinks and food near the counter. Spills can damage equipment and it's unprofessional.

The area near the checkout line needs to have some space. I would recommend at least seven to eight feet between your counter and your first display. You will need this space for people and carts to get around. Besides, your customers will take time getting through the checkout and others need space. The counter can also be a place where customers either want to gather or ask questions, slowing the process. You want to get them processed as quickly as possible to keep the line moving. I realize this isn't always possible, but every case is different. People don't like slow lines but some need information and some like to talk. This is all part of the garden center business. You'll have to get used to it. Your customers will like you and benefit from your knowledge.

The Building

Your garden center building should have enough space to comfortably display everything you need to keep dry. You'll need adequate space for all your fertilizers, chemicals, seeds, and the like. You'll need enough space for the display shelving to accommodate these too. Remember your aisle space. Don't crowd your displays; less is more. You'll need an inside storage area for surplus merchandise. This should include some shelving as well. Your backstock needs to be easy to process when needed.

You may want an area for house plants. This area needs to be well lit. This can be achieved by windows or artificial lighting. Again, make a nice, attractive, customer-friendly display. Garden giftware is popular and should be inside too. Not too many folks want rusted, faded, or otherwise unsalable merchandise. If you do get the rare customer that's interested, they'll want a discount. There goes your profit. Keep your giftware inside, dusted, priced, and displayed well. Groupings of like-type items work best—all chimes together, all rain chains together, etc. These displays should say, "I'm fun; take me home!" Good signing is essential. And again (no, I'm not done), everything needs to be priced! Your customers won't want to wait in line to find a price if something's not priced. Would you?

The Bedding Area

Your bedding area should be covered if possible. I know, I know. "Another expense!" you say. But the plants will handle the weather better and your customers will be able to shop on rainy days. In southern climates you can use shade cloth over the bedding structure as needed. Word will travel fast that your place is covered and very customer friendly. Bedding tables can be easily built from cinder blocks and planks. Pressure-treated wood works best. Remember, your plants need light. Avoid covering flats with tier-type benches. If you have to due to space issues, be sure to rotate your flats to assure plants get good light. Without rotation, plants in the back of the flats will suffer, making them unsalable. Try to avoid putting flats on the ground under benches for the same reason. This practice only works during the peak season for very short periods of time. And again, have good signing, please. An additional note: Your bedding structure will work nicely for the hanging baskets that you'll need for Mother's Day.

The Can Yard

As we discussed earlier, gravel, asphalt, and concrete are your choices here. However, some garden centers use bark. If you buy an existing place, you don't have much choice. All these have pros and cons. If I had my choice, I'd go with a hard surface such as asphalt or concrete. Hard surfaces, unlike gravel, are always level. Solid ground is easier to walk on and to pull carts across; and, unlike gravel and bark surfaces, plants will sit flat and display nicely. There doesn't seem to be any adverse conditions in terms of plant growth on any of these surfaces. I've worked at nurseries with all of them. Bark is really the least desirable. It stays soggy longer after it rains, it's uneasy to walk or pull carts on, and it's hard for customers to manage over. Plants are usually uneven in the blocks on bark and plants that are with you for long enough can root into the bark surface, reaching through drain holes on the bottom of the pots. Whatever you choose as your can yard surface, always keep your rows straight. Use a string line to achieve this. Oh yes—again, signing please!

The Tree Line

Let's face it, trees fall down. And when they do, they usually take others with them. This is like a domino effect. When this happens, it can create broken branches and blocked aisleways. The canopy is usually too large for the pot and soil to weigh them down. This can be a frustrating, ongoing problem. What to do? Some nurseries secure the pot to the ground. This makes it challenging for your customer to get. Others will tie the trees to a metal wire run laterally like a clothesline. Still others will tie them to a fence.

What I've found works best is this: Simply use bricks to weigh down the pot. It's simple, affordable, and easy for your customer to work with. You may want to have a few signs explaining this to your customers. Of course, if large canopy trees have been repotted as they mature to larger pots, this may solve the problem.

Trees should not block your front fence. A few may be brought up when they're in bloom. This is a good time to promote and possibly sell them. With the exception of spotting a few throughout your nursery, trees are usually best situated near the back of your can yard.

The Shade Area

Most garden centers will need a shade area created for shade-loving plants. The size of this area depends on how many shade-loving plants you have. A simple framework structure is good. I would recommend using fifty percent shade cloth for covering. You may want a higher percentage of shade cloth (such as eighty percent) in southern areas that are hotter and will require a higher density of shade. Shade cloth can be purchased from a garden center supply store or online. In areas that get snow, it's best to remove the cloth during the winter months. The shaded area doesn't dry out as fast as the rest of your can yard. Be aware of this and check water needs before you blanket water the area. This may end up being an every-other-day watering area.

The Transplanting Area

It's a good idea to have an area set aside for your transplanting needs. This area doesn't have to be very large. A small transplanting table should be available for up-potting smaller (two gallons or less) plants. As unsold plants mature, they will need to be repotted. This allows the plants more root room to remain healthy and keep growing. Up-potted plants are worth more money too. Don't be afraid to reprice them higher since they'll ultimately become a larger plant. Keep this area tidy. You should plan for this area in the back of your nursery, preferably out of the public eye.

The Hold Area

When customers purchase plants and don't have the means to transport them, you should offer to hold them. Large special orders and plants for landscape design all need an area to be held. Depending upon the policy you create, this holding service could be a few days up to a few weeks, or longer.

For this service, you will need a selected spot. This area should be out of public view; somewhere near the back of the store is usually preferred. Make sure to identify the owner with a sign. It's best to use flagging tape around these orders as well. These plants should be paid for before going into this area. You'll have to keep them watered and maybe spaced a bit to prevent leaf damage. Shade plants should be tucked in between taller plants if possible. Remember, you are responsible for these plants until they're picked up. That being said, I wouldn't recommend holding plants for more than a week. Also, don't hold anything smaller than a one-gallon pot size. They may be difficult to keep wet.

The Delivery Area

This area should be easily accessible for delivery trucks of all sizes. You'll want to provide enough turn-around room as well, usually near the street or preferably around the back of your place if possible. That way you're not disturbing the parking lot. This is not how my store was. I had no choice but to take deliveries in the front of the store. It didn't block the entry to the store but it upset parking until we could get the truck unloaded. Fortunately, there were seldom weekend deliveries. If I could have done it differently, I would have.

There are several other issues with the delivery area. Frequently customers will want to pick through merchandise as it's coming off the truck. This is only natural. However, the newly arriving inventory needs to be counted and priced before it can be sold. Many wholesale nurseries, however, offer pre-pricing. This makes a huge difference when it comes to processing. Some bedding plant wholesalers ship their plants on racks. This can help with the immediate display issue, but only for a short time. The shelves prevent much light for the plants, and watering is really hard. Once the racks are emptied, they need to be stored securely at your store until they come back to pick them up. This is usually the next week. This can take up valuable retail space. You need to plan ahead for this. Racks can't be left outside of your fenced areas in most cases.

The Satellite Register

You may decide to set up another register to help you move customers through faster during the busy season. Here are some things to think about: You will need to have a small shed or building with a roof over the top to keep your equipment dry. This register area will be equipped with power and all the necessary attachments for your POS system. The register will need to have an employee in it at all times. You may decide to open it on weekends only. This makes more sense, but you still need to train your customers about this method of checking out. Again, you will always need staff on hand when it's open. This is for security reasons and to keep your newly trained customers happy. The satellite building will need to be locked up at night with nothing remaining in the register. This is a good practice for any of your registers anyway.

Employee Parking

Let's say you have twenty-three parking spaces—my store did—and during the peak season you have around ten employees (full- and part-time). See the problem? This will limit your customer base immensely. Your potential customers may simply pass you by. After going to your store a few times, they may go elsewhere. Worse, word gets around quickly that there are never any parking spaces at your store. Fortunately for me, there was an empty lot next door. I contacted the owner about using it for our staff parking. I suggested renting and they said, "just keep it mowed." That was a real blessing for our business. You may scout this out ahead of time. Sometimes street parking works too, but oftentimes, busy streets don't allow parking. Ours didn't. Just be aware of this before you get started.

Carts

Your carts and wagons should have a central location in your nursery. They should always be returned to this spot as well. You want to make it easy and familiar for your customers. Plan this into your yard design. It may end up using a bit of space, but this is essential. Shopping carts are easy to find and readily available (usually) at the grocery store. Yours should be too. You don't want customers to fill a carryout tray and go home because they couldn't find a cart. It's that simple. Here are some other notes on carts worthy of mention:

1. Find carts with big tires able to navigate gravel (if your can yard surface is gravel).

2. Your carts and wagons don't all have to be the same. Some folks may prefer a smaller cart because they're easier to work with.

3. Spend the money on good carts. It pays off in the long run.

4. Keep all carts in good repair. They should be checked, cleaned, oiled, and bolts tightened regularly.

5. Replace damaged carts. If repairing doesn't work, dispose of them. Your carts will take a beating; they haul heavy things and are exposed to the weather. No customer likes a damaged cart.

Inventory

YOUR INVENTORY IS WHY YOU ARE IN BUSINESS. This is the single most important part of your shop. You need to select your inventory (all of it) very carefully. You need to be in tune and aware of this at all times. Here's where you start and what you need to know:

1. what to buy
2. what to pay
3. what to charge
4. who to buy from
5. when to buy
6. what size(s)
7. how many
8. how long the turnaround time is
9. when to rebuy
10. when to stop buying

You will need to be aware of and comfortable with these points for everything you sell. Everything. The future of your garden center inventory depends solely on these ten points. You need to know about everything you sell.

You have to buy smart to sell smart. It's that simple. You need to know the value of what you, and ultimately your customer, are getting. You truly do get what you pay for. Your customers will (and should) expect top quality from you. This is part of what separates your store from others. They'll want to see the difference.

Search out choice growers. Schedule nursery tours to be sure their quality fits your needs. Good growers may not be taking any new customers. Find all this out first. Though it's a temptation, don't sell plants that aren't for your area. This will come back to haunt you. Getting the right product mix takes time. Don't be afraid to try new things. Your customers are always looking for new and unusual plants. This sets you apart from your competitors.

Finding Your Niche

By studying your market, you should be able to see rather quickly what others are doing. The chain stores always have the same cookie cutter inventory. It's the independent stores you'll want to study. These will be your competitors. Look closely. Is their main focus bedding, shrubs, trees, or houseplants? What will you do to be different? That's the question you'll need to focus on. You'll want to carry the basics—your customers will expect this—but, besides superior quality, it's what you will do differently to stand out and be noticed that matters. Here are some ideas:

~ Pricing

Setting competitive retails is certainly the first idea in mind, but there's more to pricing than that. Remember, you get what you pay for. Therefore, your customers will always expect to pay more for quality products. If you plan to carry, say, rare and unusual plants, you can expect to charge more. New items will get a bump up over usual retail too. When you have something people want, don't be afraid to charge more. Be competitive but take your fair share. You can't make a living doubling your wholesale cost anymore. There are too many other variables to figure in. More on that later.

~ Quality

Don't be afraid to use the dumpster. If you won't buy it, nobody else will. This can't be overstated. You and your crew have to constantly be on the lookout for problem plants. Underwatered, overwatered, rootbound, and even yellow leaves can all be problems.. The plants you bring in should look as good or better than when you took them off the truck. Trust me, many nurseries aren't overly critical in this area. Being the plant police of your merchandise will always set you apart from the others. Just visit nearly any nursery after a heat wave and you'll see what I mean. Some nurseries have what is sometimes referred to as a bone yard, a place where they put stressed plants at a reduced price. My answer to this is a firm, "don't." This shows that you have a place in your garden center with lower standards. That sends a message that not all of your merchandise is up to your high-quality standards. Sometimes people will even bring back purchased plants from the bone yard claiming they died and want a refund. Just a bad idea all around. Write the plants off and throw them away. Problem solved.

Keep it Clean

You sell dirt. It can never be too clean. Constant sweeping, deadheading, and general cleanliness will set you apart. Your aisles should be free of dirt, tags, leaves, etc. Your carts should be clean and free of debris. Paint your carts once a year. All unused flats under tables in your bedding area should be returned to the bedding racks to go back to the grower on the next visit. Your can yard should be free of weeds at all times. Use a preemergent herbicide to keep weeds under control. Nothing says "yuck" like a pot full of weeds. This goes for your nursery in general. There should be no weeds anywhere. Keep them sprayed on a regular basis. You should always walk your nursery every day in the morning before you open to spot potential problems. Deadheading spent flowers is an ongoing and never-ending job that will help a plant bloom more. Untidy plants with spent blooms may never sell. Yellow leaves is another constant maintenance task. Plants with yellow leaves may never sell either. Watch your inventories carefully. Keep your inventory moving with mid-season sales on slowly moving plants. It's your money. Remember, growing plants is like farming; plants have constant needs and don't take a day off.

Price Tags

Nothing says "don't buy me" like an unpriced item. Think about it. How often has that happened to you? Irritating, isn't it? If you make a constant effort to keep everything priced, you'll sell more. It's that simple. Picture this: It's a busy Saturday. A customer is looking at a specimen-size Japanese maple. The tag used to say $499.99 but it became faded and unreadable. The customer isn't going to load the tree up, bring it up to the register, and wait in line just to get the price. Everyone seems too busy to ask. That's a sales opportunity lost. Don't let this happen to you. Replace brittle tags that have faded prices every year. This is something many of your competitors don't even think about.

Having What Your Market Wants

Aside from having inventory that sets you aside from your competitors, there's something else...needs. Here are some examples:

~ A New Neighborhood

New homeowners have one thing in common (besides a new house): dirt, and lots of it. It's a blank slate that screams "plant me, please!" Here are their needs: landscape design, soil amendments, grass seed, fertilizers, trees, and lots of shrubs. I worked at a nursery like this; you need volume.

~ An Established Neighborhood

These folks already have established landscapes. So, you ask, "What are their needs?" It's rather simple, really. Drive through the neighborhood for clues. You may see a man proudly watering his lawn. He's going to need lawn food. In the next block you see a lady planting color in her flower beds. She's going to want more color. A few blocks later you see a couple removing some overgrown shrubs from their front yard. They're going to need replacement shrubs, possibly from you if you advertised right. Let them know about your store, and that you have what they need. Simple detective work, really. You can do this.

The Fall Sale

The question remains: Is this a good idea or a not-so-good one? Let's look at the big picture. You've had a good spring and summer. Sales have been strong, but the competition always has a big fall sale with anywhere from twenty-five to fifty percent off. Should you follow them in this? After all, everyone is expecting you to. That's the big question. Remember earlier we talked about learning from your competitors, not being like them. Well, here's my take on it: don't. If your cash flow is good, there is no reason to give away your inventory. Remember, you spent the time and labor to keep it alive all summer. Besides, it's larger and worth more money than when you first brought it in. Furthermore, you're going to have to buy it again next year, and you're giving it away at cost or below. Nonsense really. I'm not sure how this whole fall sale idea started but it simply makes no sense at all. Don't be like all the others.

A Few More Thoughts

✔ Don't be afraid to send back over- or undergrown plants. This is tied up money.

✔ For large special orders, have your vendor send you pictures to show your customer. Take a deposit, maybe half down. This is a judgement call on your part.

✔ Try to get guaranteed sale (or close to) from your seed packet companies.

✔ Have a few signs around your nursery stating your plant guarantee policy. This helps promote sales. It gives peace of mind to your customers.

✔ Keep close tabs on slow-moving items. Buy less next season or maybe none at all.

✔ Don't overbuy anything. You may get stuck with it. This slow-moving inventory ties up your money.

✔ Be aware of availability shortages well in advance. You don't want to order your Mother's Day baskets the week before. They'll be long gone.

✔ Maintain a close relationship with your growers and suppliers. This is a good relationship to have. They'll go the extra mile for you.

How the Seasons Work

~ January

This is the month to prepare for the growing season. Complete all building projects, organizing, and cleaning.

~ February

The bare root stock arrives. The early planting season begins. Roses, fruit trees, small fruits, shade trees, and early bedding plants are in.

~ March

All general nursery stock arrives. Broadleaf evergreen shrubs, conifers, spring bulbs, and perennials arrive.

~ April

Showtime! The season begins in full swing. All stock is in place. Annuals arrive.

~ May

The busiest month in the business.

~ June

The busy season continues for the first half of the month. Vegetable sales slow down by the fifteenth. As the kids get out of school, the season slows down.

~ July

By the fourth, the main season rush is over. Traypak color moves into four-inch color.

~ August

Hot, dry, and slow. Many are on vacation. It's too hot and late (some feel) for planting. This is the slowest month in the business, short of January.

~ September

With school clothes bought and the kids back in school, the fall season begins. Time to plant trees and shrubs again. Fall bulbs arrive.

~ October

Fall planting is in full swing. There is less shock to plants when the weather is cool. This needs to be promoted. Fall color includes pansies, violas, mums, and flowering cabbage and kale.

~ November

Fall planting continues through the first half of the month. The last half of the month is spent preparing for the Christmas season. Benches are removed to make space for trees; plants get put out of mind for a while.

~ December

Many nurseries take advantage of the Christmas season by selling Christmas-related items—trees (cut and live), poinsettias, wreaths, arrangements, and gifts. More on this later.

You can nearly set your clock to this calendar. However, the season will shift in the south. It's important to know how your seasons work in this business, since you have a small (twelve golden weeks) window to really hit it hard; you need to be prepared. That said, all your staff should be hired and trained by the first of April. Your inventory should be signed. Your bedding benches and carts should be in good repair. You'll need to have a good inventory of cardboard carryout boxes ready for bedding season as well. Remember, when we get to showtime, there's no going back. Your focus needs to be on running your inventory out the door. This is of real importance since you don't get another chance at your twelve golden weeks. Be ready and sell!

Annuals Popularity

Annuals are most likely to be sold in traypaks. Their popularity is ranked below between 1 and 5, with 5 being the most popular.

Ageratum 2
Alyssum 5
Aster 2
Bachelor's button 2
Begonia fibrous 3
Calendula 2
Celosia 4
Coleus 3
Cosmos 4
Dahlia (border types) 3
Dusty miller 3
Gazania 3
Impatiens 5
Livingston daisy 1
Lobelia (trailing and upright) 4
Marigold 5
Mimulus 3
Nasturtium 3
Nicotiana 2
Pansy (viola) 5
Petunia 5
Phlox 2
Portulaca 4
Salpiglossis 2
Salvia 4
Schizanthus 2
Snapdragon 4
Statice 2
Stock 2
Torenia 2
Verbena (upright) 4
Vinca 2
Zinnia 5

This is merely a guide and will change by climate zones.

The Buying Shows

There are quite a few dealer supply shows that promote our industry. They are held at various times of the year (mainly October through February) and have an auditorium full of vendors that cater to the plant world. These shows are located in various regions throughout the states. Show times and locations can be found online. The gardening shows are a good place for you to find everything (or most everything) that you need for your garden center. Plants, fertilizers, giftware, and gadgets can all be found under one roof. For the new nursery, it's a good introduction to vendors and products. For the seasoned nursery person, it's a great place to go to see new vendors and merchandise. Before you go to the shows, have a good idea of what you're looking for. It's easy to get overwhelmed really quickly. The benefits, other than the merchandise, are the discounts and dating. Buy now, pay later. You will start receiving the merchandise you've ordered almost as soon as you get back! The best part is not having to pay for it for months, usually until after Mother's Day. You should have really good cash flow by then or something's wrong. Depending on the type of show, you will meet lots of plant brokers that will help you find a good variety of plants that may be new to you. Lots of the vendors will entice you to purchase by offering show specials, clearance items, and promotional goods.

Be careful not to overbuy. It's easy to get carried away. The products look great, the salespeople are smooth, and the prices and terms are attractive. You can get stuck with many impulse-buy items before you know it. If you're not careful, you can spend lots of money. Many of your purchases will most likely remain when the invoice is due. Be smart or you'll tie up your hard-earned money. Sure, you still have the product that you got for a deal, but it may not sell till next year or later. The other situation to consider is space for all your show purchases. Unless you have a large display floor, you're going to need extra space to store this extra inventory. Some nurseries have a storage room; I did. Others will store their extra merchandise at home in their garage. Both of these seem ideal; however, your buying public won't see them. Whatever you choose, be smart, keep your inventory moving, and don't overbuy.

Chemicals

HOW MANY TIMES HAVE YOU WALKED through a garden center to see someone staring blindly at the chemical display? This is a cry for help that can't happen at your store. Your customer rarely knows this stuff. It's up to you and your crew to answer their questions. Chemicals and fertilizer knowledge must be mastered and taught to both your crew and your customers. Chemicals and fertilizers should be a big part of your business. You can't stay in business just selling plants. Your chemical and fertilizer line is an instant tie-in sale. Sell a plant and sell the food to go along with it. It's that simple.

That said, you want to sell a brand your customer can only purchase from you, not a brand they can buy just anywhere. This builds loyalty. (More on this later.) You also don't want to have competing items either. Having five different types of slug bait simply confuses your customer. Keeping it simple makes it easier for your customers and your staff to understand.

You're the Expert

Your customers come to you seeking answers to their gardening questions. At times I would have three or more customers waiting for me to solve their plant problems in a plastic bag. This was a regular occurrence. You have the answers they need and they're willing to wait their turn.

Following a brief discussion, select the right product off the shelf for them. Put it in their hand and begin explaining. You must sound believable to your customer. Never guess. Never say "I think;" it means you're unsure. Instead, read the label with your customer. This way, you're sure. Your customer will appreciate your honesty if you don't know mixing rates or something else. In time, you and your crew will get familiar with dilution rates of many chemicals. Soon, this will become part of your daily routine. As you get more comfortable with troubleshooting and product selection, you'll be able to pick a product off the shelf, put it in their hand, and say, "This is what you need." Always explain in detail the application rates and frequency of the selection. Remember, your customer trusts your selection. In time word travels that you're the local expert. Also, training your crew about chemicals and plant foods will benefit you greatly. It's just one more part of building your reputation through knowledge and understanding.

Knowing Your Products

Product knowledge meetings with your crew are really important. The more information you pass on to your staff, the easier your job becomes. Group topics that address current issues are always beneficial. Keep your crew informed whenever possible.

Topics like lawn care and rose care should be common knowledge with your crew. Seasonal discussions, such as dormant spraying, weed control, and fertilizer usage, will help your crew feel more comfortable with chemical and fertilizer knowledge. This sells more product for your store. You should begin your introduction to the chemical world to your staff with the basics. Fertilizer analysis and uses is a great place to begin. Weed control, pesticides, and fungicides should follow. Keep your training simple and easy to understand. With so much to know and understand in this department, basic information works best. You'll be able to tell after a few product knowledge meetings just how much information is good, and what's too much. Again, simple, basic knowledge is where you start. Some vendors will offer product knowledge meetings with your staff. They can schedule times and days that work for your crew. Take advantage of this opportunity! Your representatives are the best resource you have.

You Feed Your Kids, Don't You?

Introducing your customers to the world of chemicals can be challenging. Simply said, you have to teach it to them in ways they'll understand. All sales situations (and customers) are uniquely different. This is where reading your customer as you're selecting plants, for instance, is good. You'll be studying how receptive they'll be with your potential tie-in additions while you're in the yard. This is also where you begin the conversation of the need for root stimulator, planting mix, fertilizer, etc. Most often, when people trust you, tie-ins are easier. However, not all your customers will know you. Again, establishing trust through explaining the importance of what you're proposing as a tie-in is vital. In a perfect set up, your customers (and carts of plants) will pass right by your endcap of tie-ins. This is your chance. It's really easy. You stop the cart in front of the display and begin "You'll need this, and this," and so on. Not only are you making sales, you're helping your customer succeed. I once had a saleswoman that taught me a great idea. I had taught her the virtues and reasons to use Fertilome Bloom and Root fertilizer weekly on flowering plants. Knowing this, she stocked around ten cases behind the counter before the annual Mother's Day basket rush. Each time a customer would come to the counter with a basket, she would set a bottle on the counter. Then she would say, "You need this!" If she was met with resistance at all, she would say, "I can't sell you the basket without the plant food." Brilliant! Some customers bought several. Others bought larger sizes. That's a great sales trick. But who really wins here? Your customer.

Explaining the Product

The idea here is simple. It begins with a fine-tip permanent marker. You'll want to have a few of these at a certain spot near your chemical display. It's actually best to carry one with you during the day; here's why: When you begin to explain the usage of the chemical or fertilizer, mark the bottle for them then put it in their hand. Once it's marked and in their hand, it's theirs. But there's another idea. Mark the date you're selling it on the bottle. While doing this, explain that everyone has a shed full of chemicals that are outdated and have lost their potency. Explain to your customer that it's best to keep opened bottles for only eighteen months. This way they'll get a new one from you. Suggest writing down your instructions on paper for your customer and include your phone number. Encourage them to call you with any questions. This is simply good customer service.

Organics

If you're old enough to remember, organics seemed to be set in a past generation's garden. In reality, organics are the trend of the future. This is especially true with the younger set, namely young families. The generation after us old nursery folks wants to organically grow and control everything possible. It used to be that organics were more or less overlooked. Well, that's all changed. Organics are no longer being passed over or overlooked at all. In many instances, they are preferred. The organic line of products is a must-have for all garden centers. You're really missing out if you don't have them. This is especially true because the younger families we've talked about will be your future customers for many years to come. You don't want to lose them if you don't have what they're looking for. That's just good business. There are organic fertilizers, pesticides, fungicides, and herbicides. There's a fertilizer, and control, for nearly every situation. Be sure to sign your displays well to promote them.

Shelf Talkers

Here we go again on the signing issue. If you put a brief (three to five words) sign in front of each of your chemicals, your sales will jump. I did this at my store and was pleasantly surprised. The last thing the independent nursery owner wants is to have the store considered self-serve. This just makes good sense. You and your crew can't be everywhere; this we know. Signs really help explain things in your absence. Your customers will appreciate the guidance. Remember, you can't expect your customers to know what you do. This simply just helps them out. A few simple words do wonders. For instance, write "I turn hydrangeas blue" on your aluminum sulfate display.

Island Displays

Nothing says "buy me" more than an island display of, well, anything. The best application of this in your nursery will most likely be a large display of fertilizer or another popular bagged product. A big display says that you recommend the product. This can be further spelled out with signing, of course. You'll want to be sure your display targets the season you're in. Be sure to fully educate your crew on the featured product too. Have your staff promote the displayed item. You may consider an in-store promotional contest between crew members as well. The staff member that sells the most product from the display wins. You can make the prize anything that sounds attractive, like a one-hundred-dollar bill, movie passes, or dinner at a local pizza pub. This promotion could go for a few weeks or months; it's your call. These sale contests are fun for your crew. You may consider promoting a different product each month. Try it. You'll sell more product than you knew you could. We did.

Voluntary Purchasing Groups (VPG)

This is the product company you'll want for your business. They sell to only independent garden centers, never to box stores. This gives you a huge competitive edge. Your customers can get the products from only you. This, of course, keeps them coming back. This company is seriously a one-stop shop too. They carry an impressive line of about everything you'll need to sell. They've got great pricing and top-quality products. Some of their inventory includes a full line of fertilizers, pesticides, fungicides, herbicides, slug bait, organics, soils, and houseplant foods, just to name a few. I even get my carryout trays from them! They have everything you need. This makes your job easy. Let's face it, you have a lot to do every day. That's an understatement. This company will take a world of stress off your plate by having everything you need in one company. Their representatives will do product knowledge seminars with your staff too. They've done many for me through the years. There's nothing better for your staff and you than to let a factory representative explain their product.

Here's a look at the company's early order incentive program:

ferti·lome   **ferti·lome**   **Hi-Yield**

Dealer Early Order Incentive Program

The only true early-order booking program in America for independently-owned merchants!

Earn up to a 20% cash incentive on every qualifying booking written!

AMOUNT OF ORDER	EARLY ORDER INCENTIVE
Over $25,000 (Drop Shipment)	Pays 20% Cash Incentive (10% from VPG, Inc. & up to 10% from Distributor)*
$15,000-$24,999 (Drop Shipment)	Pays 15% Cash Incentive (10% from VPG, Inc. & up to 5% from Distributor)*
$6,500-$14,999	Pays 7% Cash Incentive
$1,500-$6,499	Pays 5% Cash Incentive

But there's more to this company. VPG is a 100 percent patron-owned manufacturer, which means you have control over the company's direction. The company offers a very generous patronage refund program.

How the program works: At the end of each fiscal year in October, VPG distributors submit a patronage refund based on VPG's profits for that year. Usually in February of each year, patronage refunds are sent to the originating VPG distributor to be delivered to each dealer. Dealer patronage refunds are paid in eighty percent VPG stock ($1.05 per share) and twenty percent cash until a dealer acquires 5,600 shares of stock. At that point a dealer is vested. Once a dealer is vested, patronage refunds are paid in 100 percent cash.

So, as you can see, the more you buy (which is easy), the more you get back! This is a perfect fit for any retail garden center. I've been with them for decades. Each year the patronage refund check pays for a nice (and well needed, I might add) vacation for my family. These are the people to know for all your chemical, fertilizer, organics (and more) needs. I highly recommend VPG. They are the bottom line to your bottom line. Contact them at:

Voluntary Purchasing Groups
230 FM87, Bonham, Texas 75418-8629
Phone (903) 583-5501 Fax (888) 958-3634
or visit www.fertilome.com

Additional Notes

- At least one person (besides you) should be knowledgeable about fertilizer and chemical usage.
- Have seasonal chemicals and fertilizers on your endcaps.
- Teach your staff about the importance of these products.
- Introduce a product every week to your staff.
- Have product knowledge meetings often.
- These products are an essential tie-in.
- Every plant sale should leave with something extra.

Your Staff

YOUR STAFF REPRESENTS YOU. No crew, no you. It's that simple. Many volumes have been published about this topic. I'm going to simplify it for you as it relates to the nursery business. This business is very different from most retail operations. You work outside in all types of weather; you're on your feet all day; you have to be knowledgeable about plants, soils, and chemicals; and you have to be able to troubleshoot. These are all expected from your staff. This is in addition to all the usual aspects in retail.

The Interview

1. Get the candidate to open up, get comfortable.
2. Ask, "Why do you want to work here?"
3. Display the job description.
4. "Any special skills that would help with the job?"
5. "Any restrictions or limitations? Able to lift forty pounds?"
6. "Any problems with working outside?"
7. "Any plant knowledge?"
8. Give a nursery tour and invite questions.
9. Give basic area descriptions (bedding, transplanting, etc.). Keep it simple.

10. Explain your expectations.
11. Explore wage needs—raises are by merit. Benefits?
12. Explain that the job can be seasonal. Mention employee discounts.
13. Explain that they will be learning a lot.

This is a format for a simple garden center interview. You can tell a lot about a potential hire by how they react to you. Be a good listener. Ask lots of questions, but try to let them do the talking. Hire only when you need the help. It's completely on you to train your staff. You have to lead by example if you want it to work. Remember, customer service is why your customers come to you. Expect this from your staff. It's about earning your customers' trust. Here are some things to impress on your staff:

1. Make yourself available to your customer.
2. Greet your customer within one minute.
3. Customers pick up your energy in ten to fifteen seconds.
4. Don't give the impression you're too busy to help.
5. Don't meet the public when eating, smoking, or chewing gum.
6. Body language is important. No crossed arms. Make eye contact.
7. Don't know? Ask. Remember, you're building trust.
8. Learn a plant a day.
9. Ask lots of questions and listen to the answers.
10. Wear proper attire. Come dressed for the weather: waterproof shoes, raingear, hat, gloves, etc.

Teaching Your Staff

If you don't teach your crew about the business, it's all on you. You have enough to do every day already. Besides, you hired them to help you. Teaching is an important part of your job. You'll want to have PK (product knowledge) meetings at least once a month with your entire staff. Have them punch in early. Pay them for their time. The meetings should be held before your store opens. Provide coffee and donuts. Meetings should be no more than one hour. Stay to topic. It's your money.

It's a good idea to pull staff members aside for a few minutes from time to time for a quick lesson. They'll appreciate the effort on your part and the knowledge. Your crew needs to progress at a decent rate. Again, it's about your ability to teach and lead by example. Otherwise, every day is the first day. You don't want this. Your business can't afford this. Your customers will search for you. Aim high and surround yourself with winners. Understand your employees' strengths and weaknesses. Focus on the positive in every case. Commend every job well done. You'll get more out of your crew this way.

Hiring Family

Hiring family members may seem like the right thing to do. They share your passion, drive, and ambition, right? Sorry, it's not always that way. The fact is, it seldom is that way. The passion for this business came from your love of the industry. Your drive and ambition are all from your desire to succeed. Family members can sometimes seem like hired help with some extra conditions. Family members may feel they are entitled to special privileges since they're related to you. Longer breaks, special work hours, and extra time off are a few. They may also feel they are above others in seniority. They may feel they're an extension of you when guiding the staff.

Don't get me wrong, you may want this. It is, however, worth mentioning here. Things can get a bit awkward, in fact quite ugly, when you have a family member overstepping their bounds by telling others what to do if this isn't their position to begin with. If you have two family members working with you and one quits, you may lose both. I've seen this happen. It can really put a strain on your family. Worse, you may lose other staff members too. Sometimes, however, family members will work into the business perfectly. They may even take over your garden center when you're ready to retire. These are simply words of caution from experience.

More Stuff

✔ Limit personal friendships with staff members. Everyone wants to be your friend. Keep it professional. Keep it at work. I've seen owners that become friendly with staff outside of work. It's hard for these crew members to take you seriously anymore. Again, like family members, they may feel entitled to special privileges as listed before. Be wise with this.

✔ Be aware of personal conflicts staff members may have with one another. Let's face it, we're all different. But somehow, we all need to be the same when it comes to working for the shop and the goals and commitments that make up the team. Sometimes one employee may not like another and lets it be known. This conflict may blow over in time. Sometimes it's just a matter of not liking the new guy, because, well, he's new. In other cases it becomes an issue that needs to be dealt with before it becomes a problem with your entire crew taking sides and talking behind each other's backs. In some cases crew may leave. You don't want this. The easiest way to deal with this is the old grade school approach in the principal's office. Before problems escalate, bring the two into your office and hash it out. Seems juvenile, but it works.

✔ Sexual Harassment is something that's not to be tolerated in any way, shape, or form. Even the most subtle offences will be taken seriously. Have a zero tolerance on this one.

✔ Employee theft. Did you know that over fifty percent of your shrinkage is from your staff? A crazy statistic, but true. Here again, have a zero tolerance.

✔ Involve your team when trying to formulate new ideas. Everyone sees things differently. And different backgrounds can help you with new ideas. Remember, you're in the box. Your crew is thinking outside of the box. This can make for some really great ideas and practices to put in place. How many times have we said, "Why didn't I think of that?" It's just because none of us see things the same. Use your crew to your advantage. They want to help, are paid to help, so let them. Brainstorming sessions are really a great way to resolve issues and create new ideas.

✔ Provide a monthly or two-week review for all new employees. At the end of the two weeks with your business, just have a brief meeting. This way you can answer questions they may have. It's also a good time to give a mild progress report. You can offer areas of improvement. "I like how you're working; we just need to work on speed." You can even offer, "I'm aware this comes in time". That way it's been said and hope the point was taken. It's also a good time to ask them how they like the job so far. You may even open the conversation with this. Be sure to offer praise when you can.

Projects

A good garden center doesn't function efficiently or effectively without tasks. In fact, the entire day is a project, large and small. The biggest task is sales, of course. From unloading delivery trucks to watering to deadheading spent blooms, there's always something to do. If an employee tells you otherwise, you're not doing your job. It's up to you and management to set up the tasks of the day (other than sales, certainly) and see they're done in a timely manner. Projects are like pieces of a puzzle. When the day is done, the puzzle should be complete.

The To-Do List

In order to stay on top of everything, you need a list. Trying to remember everything is just too hard. Besides, you need to prioritize your tasks and those for your crew. The list should be updated constantly and new items added on a daily (or nearly) basis. Make sure your crew knows exactly what you want done, and how. You have to take the time to teach or demonstrate what you want done. Be clear. Be sure they understand completely. If it's done wrong, it's on you. Don't assume they know this stuff; most times they don't. Be sure not to overload your crew with projects because it's easy to become overwhelmed. It's best to demonstrate only three projects at a time. This may be a bit more work for you, but they'll understand a few projects rather than a whole day's worth. After you've created the current to-do list, keep it near your desk on a clipboard. Initial and date the project when you're giving it. Follow up to be sure it's done to your liking, then cross it off. Your staff member should feel responsible for this task. They should be corrected if it's not done right. Some explanation should follow on both your and their part. Keeping your eyes open at all times is an important part of the to-do list. Remember, there's always cleaning, deadheading, sweeping, or removing yellow leaves. As mentioned, it's a good idea to keep your to-do list near your desk so you can add things as you think of them. If you keep the list in the breakroom, your crew may gather around it, wondering what the project means and otherwise wasting your time. It's best to explain each job to the intended crew member. If necessary, write the three projects on a piece of paper with the crew member's name at the top. It serves as a reminder to them if necessary.

20-50-90

Here's a trick I picked up somewhere along the way. It's a useful tool that has worked well for me. Here's how it works: After assigning a task, check with the employee after twenty percent of the job should be completed for understanding and accuracy. After fifty percent of the task should be completed, a follow through on your part should be done. This allows the employee freedom, which is important. No one likes to be monitored. After ninety percent of the job should be completed, follow up again. Be certain the task is complete to your satisfaction. This is your chance to make any last necessary adjustments. Be sure to commend their work when possible. Everyone likes a pat on the back now and then. This helps build confidence and morale. You'd be surprised how well this works. This is especially useful for new hires and for projects that may be a bit complex.

Some Final Thoughts

- ✔ You may want to create an employee learning manual. Limit it to the basics.
- ✔ Have every crew member be responsible for an area in the nursery. This may help you stay better organized.
- ✔ Name tags may be an idea to identify all your staff members.
- ✔ When it comes to time off, ask your crew to be fair. It slows production and sales when staff is missing. Other employees have to cover for them besides doing their own work. Remember, they were hired to work. Limit times off during April and May.
- ✔ Cell phone usage should be limited. Sure, Google is a great sales tool to display plants' blooms, shapes, etc., but employees want to use their phones for personal things. This reduces productivity. We had our crew leave their phones in their lockers; problem solved.
- ✔ Don't hire anyone that doesn't fit your plan.
- ✔ Always have a spring in your step. Your crew should do the same.
- ✔ Always expect the unexpected from your crew. Don't be disappointed with the outcome.
- ✔ Have your crew clean up the area they were working in at least ten minutes before the end of their shift. No one likes to come back to a mess the next day.

Employee Handbook Ideas

- ☐ Equal Opportunity Employer
- ☐ Sexual Harassment
- ☐ At-Will Employee
- ☐ Drug Free
- ☐ Dress Code
- ☐ Work Performance Expectations
- ☐ Excessive Late to Work/Absences
- ☐ Safety Issues
- ☐ Sick Pay
- ☐ What's Expected of Our Workers
- ☐ Exit Interview
- ☐ Company Discount
- ☐ Employee-Employee Relations

Garden Center Learning Guide

Below are some general ideas that may help you to create a learning guide for your staff. I created one for my garden center. I went through a chapter every week during our staff meetings. I believe it helped my crew better understand the retail garden center business.

- ✔ How Plants Grow
- ✔ Annuals
- ✔ Perennials
- ✔ Trees
- ✔ Shrubs
- ✔ Vines
- ✔ Ground Covers
- ✔ Herbs
- ✔ Fruits and Vegetables
- ✔ Shade Gardening
- ✔ Fertilizers and Chemicals
- ✔ Soil Preparation
- ✔ Proper Planting

- Watering
- Organics
- Pruning
- Plants for Hot or Dry Spots
- Flowers for Cutting
- Deer-Proof Plants
- Espaliers
- Attracting Bees
- Lawns
- Hedging Plants
- Roses

There are so many topics to teach your crew. The area in which you live will certainly yield more ideas.

Employee Basic Job Description

- days and hours scheduled
- breaks and lunches
- clothing—come prepared and provide your own raingear
- on your feet all day—wear comfortable shoes
- safety—if something is too heavy, get help
- sales
- unloading trucks
- processing inventory
- pricing
- transplanting
- watering
- cleaning
- register
- monthly safety meetings
- monthly product knowledge meetings
- constant learning

Caring for Living Inventory

TAKING CARE OF LIVING THINGS is no different whether they're animals or plants. You've chosen plants. Plants have the same basic needs. They're all living things that need food, water, and tending to. Plants, in your situation, will need constant attention. Some will need more than others, such as bedding plants. Constant grooming, spacing, feeding, and watering are the norm. As with everything in your store, constant attention is required. Plants are the biggest attention getters. Sure, you can put plants on a table and water them now and then, but you don't want to be like other nurseries. You want to excel, to set yourself apart from all your competitors. To do this, special attention needs to be paid to all your living inventory. I remember my mentor telling me, "Anyone can sell plants. We sell quality; just look around." Remember, you're not "anyone." Your buying public notices the difference. This is what you strive for and this is what you want to be known for.

Proper Exposure

Perhaps nothing makes a plant more upset than being put in the wrong exposure. Visit big box stores and you'll find impatiens frying in the sun and geraniums stretching for light in the shade. All plants have needs; proper lighting is the most critical. You have to pay close attention to this. You have to teach, then monitor, your crew about proper plant exposure.

It really doesn't take long for a plant to show problems if it's set in the wrong environment. If not addressed quickly, the damage may be irreversible. It's just that important. Tender bedding plants are the most vulnerable to adverse conditions. It doesn't take long for bedding to show signs of struggling. Sun plants almost instantly stop blooming in the shade and shade plants put into a sun setting on a hot summer day may be unsalable within a day. Shade-loving shrubs put into a sun setting are a bit more forgiving, but this still needs to be corrected as soon as possible. Hot summer sun can scorch leaves quickly. Once burned leaves are removed, the plant may not be salable until next year. Keep a close eye on proper plant exposure at all times. A new staff member may be unaware of the situation.

Spacing

Bedding plants arrive "pot tight" in flats. Unless the plants are relatively small (foliage not touching foliage), they should be spaced. As a general rule, each flat you have (Traypaks excluded) should be divided into two flats. This does two things. It fills your benches faster and, more importantly, gives the plants some breathing room. Without spacing, plants left in the shipping flat will begin to yellow at the edges and stretch for light.

Good spacing also reduces damage caused by customers pulling plants out of the flats. So, the spacing of bedding plants is considered essential. The spacing of shrubs is a good idea too. When you get your deliveries of inventories in the spring, it's really easy to put plants "can tight" just to fit everything in. That's typical in the nursery trade. It's hard to spend time spacing your inventory with so much going on. Your crew has moved on to other priorities, such as bedding and customer service. You'll have to make an effort to begin spacing as soon as you're able. Maybe put one team member on the task. It doesn't take a lot of explaining but it is necessary. Shrubs left "can tight" through the season will end up growing together. This prevents the sun from hitting the entire plant. The result is yellowing leaves and most likely tender growth on branches that haven't seen sunlight. These branches may have to be removed if left for too long. In some cases, this damage may make the plant unsalable. The other reasons for spacing are keeping good inventory counts and for ease of watering. It's hard to find the right pot to water when plants are too close together. If you keep spacing a priority, you'll have healthier plant stock. As a footnote, trees will benefit from spacing too, especially the evergreens.

Pruning

Pruning is an art that's learned over time. The longer you're in the business, the easier this becomes. Knowing when to prune is important for the plants. Regenerating new growth and creating new flowers is what pruning is all about. If you have plants that have overwintered at your nursery, chances are they'll need to be pruned. If plants aren't rootbound, and they're ready to be repotted, then pruning will keep the plant salable for another year in the same pot. If plants are being repotted, pruning is still a good idea to keep the plant compact in the new pot. Again, knowing how to prune, and when, will come to you with experience. Here's a general guide:

Bedding Plants

It's really more about deadheading than pruning to keep plants salable. Bedding plants usually sell quickly and don't get leggy. They should be small enough when delivered to you to have a reasonable shelf life without pruning. Petunias are one of the few that grow really fast and may need to be cut back. They'll resprout and be salable in about two weeks. So don't order heavy on petunias; go through them. Let your grower hold onto them until you're ready for more.

Broadleaf Evergreens

These are best pruned once they've finished blooming. This creates new growth and keeps the plants compact. Without some light pruning after blooming, plants may become untidy and be slow to sell.

Deciduous Shrubs

This one varies a bit. Early season bloomers such as forsythia and magnolias should not be pruned until they're done blooming. Summer bloomers can be pruned upon arrival in spring to keep the plants compact. They'll have time to generate flower buds after that.

Evergreen Shrubs (Conifers)

If any pruning is needed it's best done in the late summer before the last growth push of the year. If needed, you can also prune in very early spring, just before the spring growth.

Fruit Trees

Pruning in midwinter is best. When your new tree order arrives in late winter, the trees may need some limbing up to create a strong canopy. This should be all they need.

These are the basic groups that will need some attention. Pruning times may vary by climate zone.

Feeding

As mentioned earlier, plants need food. Without proper nourishment, plants, both in pots and in the ground, can struggle. Containerized plants have only the nutrients in the soil, or in the fertilizer from their previous nursery, to survive. Watering, of course, leaches these nutrients away. Without being replenished, plants start to have problems like slowed growth, yellow leaves, disease, and insect troubles. This is why it's important to keep your living inventory fed. It's relatively simple. Bedding plants are the most needy. Granted, they sell fast, so it's good to keep them looking good while they're on your tables. Remember, anyone can sell plants. You sell quality. So, with that being said, you'll want to have a feeding program in place. Find a day of the week that's going to work. Mondays are usually good. It's sort of a pick-up-after-the-weekend day anyway. I would suggest assigning one staff member to this task. Each week you'll want to feed your entire bedding area with a water-soluble plant food. It really doesn't take long. The result for the time spent is well worth it. This practice should run from spring through late summer. As far as shrubs and trees go, feed them twice a year with a slow-release granule-type plant food. This is best applied in early spring and again in midsummer. This changes a little by climate zone.

Rootbound Plants

When plants spend too long in their current pot, they become rootbound. These plants are under stressful conditions and need to be addressed. For the short term, you'll need to make sure to keep them watered. This needs to happen several times a day during the spring and summer. These plants need to be prevented from falling over too. The less stress, the better. Many nurseries don't pay attention to this and the plants fail. It doesn't take long for a neglected rootbound plant to perish. Keep a watch for this constantly. The longer a plant stays at your store, the more likely this is to happen. But this isn't exactly a bad thing. As previously mentioned, by shifting these plants to a larger pot, the plant will again flourish. That's only part of the beauty of this. These plants become worth more money. In many cases, they become quite a bit more money. Transplanting is (or should be) a common practice at garden centers. Sure, it's all about preserving quality, but let's face it, you're in this to make money. This becomes the best of both worlds. You've saved a plant from ultimate demise and made more money at the same time. Some nurseries, like my own, would transplant a good portion of overwintered stock to larger pots during the slow winter months. This way the crop goes into the next spring in good shape, and you've added instant profit. Of course you'll need to have a transplanting area for this. You'll also need an assortment of pots in various sizes too. Always remember to loosen the roots on plants to be repotted and keep your soil levels at least one inch from the top of the pot. You'll want to keep soil levels even lower on larger pots.

Weed Control

Weeds in the ground at your nursery should not exist. I know that's difficult. Some of your vendors don't practice this well. Once they become integrated with your stock, it is a challenge to catch them. To begin with, every plant that enters your place should be checked for weeds. They need to be pulled before they make it to your can yard. Several times a year a preemergent herbicide should be applied to the top of the soil of all your shrubs and trees to prevent weed seed from germinating. This can be sourced from a nursery supply company. Weeds in the group should be kept under control too. Nothing says "untidy" like weeds between shrubs or under benches. Again, a preemergent herbicide will keep them down. Spray with a postemergence herbicide as necessary.

Plants in Displays

As previously mentioned, care should be taken when selecting plants to be used in displays. Be sure to select colorful, interesting plants. Then comes the care part. Plants used in your displays should be kept in top form at all times. Plants that have finished blooming must be removed and replaced with ones in bloom. There should be no exceptions to this. Displays are looked upon as a reflection of your nursery. They must be attention getters at all times. You'll also want them to be available to your customers. This being said, don't make plants hard to access. After all you want to sell them. I would also recommend changing them out every week for the interest to continue. Care must also be taken when watering. Try to avoid watering the flowers but be sure to water the soil. This can be a bit challenging when displays are created with plants touching.

Large Bench Displays

A large display of one type of plant looks impressive. In order for this to work, the selected plants should be uniform and with no spent blooms. Constant grooming and deadheading are a must. Again, weekly feeding of a water-soluble plant food will help create continued and repeat blooming. Don't allow your displays to run out of charm. As soon as you feel the plants are near the end of their bloom cycle, put the display on sale and move another display into its place after two weeks. No more. A mid-season sale lasting no longer than two weeks helps you reduce inventory and get something out of the crop. Everyone loves a sale. Remember, you need to be on top of this. Know when to put the display on sale. Have another crop ready to replace this crop when the time comes.

Watering

Proper watering is an art that's learned over time. There is a science behind it. Including:

- How do I water?
- When do I water?
- How much water does each plant get?
- How often do I water?
- Which plants need more, and which take less?

These are all important questions you'll need to teach your staff how to answer before turning them loose on the hose. You'll have to impress the importance of this to everyone. Always have the crew water first in the morning, preferably before noon. Projects can, and should, happen after watering. Again, if any crew member ever doubts this, just visit any competitor after a heat wave. Enough said.

When

Always survey the area you're planning to water first for any dry spots. Water the dry plants first. Continue watering the area as usual. Then return to water the stressed plants once again. If plants are wilting badly, put them under the bench for the day. During hot spells always start watering as early in the day as possible. Plan to water again during the day. Plants with limited soil space may need additional water. During cold snaps you'll want to make sure all plants have been watered before the cold hits. Freezing weather will draw water out of the soil, then from the plant. They can ultimately freeze-dry. Of course, extra protection may be necessary. The wind will dry plants out quickly. This being said, you may find your crew will need to water again on windy days. On rainy days, don't forget to water under covered areas. This is an easy spot to forget. Plants in bloom will require more water too. Keep this in mind and pass it on. One last note for the "when" department. Some growers will ship their plants dry. This is sometimes because the plants were loaded for delivery the day before and missed watering. Always water the plants before putting them away.

Being Careful

It's been said that if you miss watering a plant on a hot day, it's dead. Is this true? Well, sort of. Some plants can take hot and dry conditions better than others. But you really have to be very complete when watering during hot spells.

Next, water and flowers don't mix. Moisture shortens the blooming on many flowering plants. It's important to keep water off flowers when plants are in bloom. This is difficult, but nonetheless a good way to prolong blooming.

Another area of concern is missing the plants in the back of the flats when watering. This is a common mistake made by new waterers. Traypak and four-inch flats are often placed on shelves with another tier above, making it a bit challenging to water the plants in the back of the flats. Be sure to teach this when introducing a new hire to watering.

Water pressure and water application are also areas of concern. Always water with a soft rain-type water breaker nozzle. This will deliver enough water without damaging plants. Water pressure should be reduced when watering bedding plants. A further reduced water pressure should be practiced when watering delicate or very young seedlings. Deep soaking is a practice that must be demonstrated to anyone with a hose. Again, this takes some time to master. A nursery person should be aware of plants' water needs before setting out to water.

On hot days you'll want to water most everything even if it's moist from the day before. This is referred to as blanket watering. There are only a few exceptions to this, such as the cacti family. Watering whether it needs it or not will keep the plant as moist as it should be on hot days. It takes twice as long to water if plants are dry. Touching off water levels in the soil will save a lot of time with the hose. Don't wait until it dries out.

For regular seasonal watering you'll want to teach your crew about the color of the soil in the top of the pot. Brown soil means the plant needs water. Black soil means the plant has water and is using it slowly.

Another note on cautious watering: When young (tender) plants first come out of a greenhouse, they must be "hardened off." This practice acclimatizes plants into a new environment. Some young plants, often vegetables, will come from your grower while still tender. This usually happens during the busy rush of spring when growers are having a hard time keeping up and they send plants young. These plants will require some extra care. First, be careful with the water pressure. It's easy to knock young plants over in this condition. Also, it's a good idea to use a misting bottle on the young plants a few times a day until the plants can adjust to the outdoor environment.

Extra Notes on Watering

- Water the pot, not the plant.
- A quick misting on a hot day after watering will slow the plants' transpiration rate.

✔ Keep the hoses out of the aisles.

✔ Have a few watering cans filled and under bedding tables for quick spot watering as needed.

✔ Wilted plants should not be on your tables. Keep them under benches until they bounce back. This was mentioned prior but it is of utmost importance.

✔ Practice keeps hose water off your feet and in the pot.

Potted Plants' Water Needs in Summer

Above Average
Rootbound plants
Fuchsias
Most deciduous trees
Willows
Water garden plants
Bedding plants
Bonsai
Angel's-trumpet
Hydrangeas
Mints

Below Average
Most conifers
Tuberous begonias
Sedum, sempervivums and succulent families
Portulaca family
Cacti
Araucaria
Grasses
Daphne
Ice plant family

These are only a few of the popular plants at many garden centers. Many plants are considered either drought tolerant or moisture lovers. This list is only for plants in pots.

The Horticultural Inspector

A horticultural inspector will visit your garden center from time to time. This inspection is usually performed once a year or more. They may come alone or with a team. The inspection may last several hours or days. Consider this team as another set of eyes in your nursery. They are trained to search out issues you may be overlooking. It's really helpful to have their expertise. Upon completion of their inspection, you'll receive a report. This report will spell out issues they have found that must be addressed. They will do a follow-up inspection to be sure you have taken the steps necessary to fix the problems. Some of the issues they'll be looking for are:

- healthy plant stock
- complying with all regulations
- necessary certifications for all certified plant material
- invasive species
- proper labeling on all plants
- insect and disease issues
- origin of plant materials, if needed
- quarantines and certifications
- proper growing conditions
- proper sanitation in all areas
- samples for analysis
- spraying records

Remember, these inspectors are on your side. They're helping you (and your store) with issues that directly impact your inventory.

Sales

HOW MANY TIMES have you walked through a store without being greeted, let alone being asked if you need help? Don't, and I repeat, don't, let this happen in your store! Your customer should be greeted within one minute of entering your store. Customer service is what it's all about. Remember that plants are a luxury to many of your customers. They have chosen your store rather than your competitor's. Reward them by being friendly and attentive. Listen to your customers. Learn from them. Be excited *with* your customer. They're likely to buy more when they're doing something that makes them happy. Be excited *for* your customers' purchases. Saying, "I love these," will help increase your sales and bring yourself to their side. It works.

The public can tell when you or your crew don't know the answer to a question. The simple rule–don't know, ask. Your customers will appreciate your honesty. Confidence, like trust, is built over time. Always be honest, upbeat, and positive. Your customers will expect you to be friendly, attentive, and willing to direct or answer questions as needed. Remember, it's up to you to train and teach your crew to be good salespeople. Without this your customers may go elsewhere.

Creating Pricing

Coming to terms with a pricing strategy can be challenging. Scouting the competition is a place to start, but as I've mentioned, you don't want to use your competitors to set your pricing. Within reason, consider yourself in a league of your own. Base your pricing on quality, service, selection, and value. Some items will certainly be good buys to yield a nice return. Other items, maybe not so much. Remember, you're all about buying smart to sell smart. Bedding plants will most likely be your fastest, and most competitive, item. Keep this in mind when setting your pricing. Bedding is what you see in the box stores and grocery stores of the world. You'll have to be as competitive as possible in this area. Most other items in your inventory will bring a comfortable return. The general rule for pricing used to be simply doubling the wholesale cost. However, there are other factors that come into play when setting your pricing. These are:

- ✔ freight
- ✔ labor
- ✔ water charges
- ✔ other utilities and general overhead
- ✔ mortgage/rental charges
- ✔ credit card processing
- ✔ taxes
- ✔ advertising, signing, and more

In setting your pricing, remember that all these factors have to come into play. With the exception of the ever popular (and competitive) bedding area, most of your inventory should be marketed at a markup of 2.25%. This covers most costs without looking too greedy or overpriced to your customer. You're simply covering your costs. These are real costs and can't be overlooked. If you do, it will catch up to you in the end. And I mean "end." It can break you.

Your larger items, such as specimen trees, should be valued at quite a bit more. The same holds true for specialty and unusual inventory. Within reason, you can set your price on items others don't carry. Be careful. Be smart. Don't price yourself out of business. Be fair to your customer. Be fair to yourself.

Raising Prices

As your costs increase so should your retail pricing. It's that simple. As previously mentioned, you can't absorb these price increases. It's all around us, actually. Gas, food, labor. It's all moving up. So, unfortunately, must you. In the beginning of each season this must be revisited. This is also the best period to do this since your season has yet to begin. By raising prices softly, they're seldom noticed. Most of your customers won't remember what they paid for plants last year. You'll need to continue being fair with pricing, certainly. Though I'm an advocate for not letting your competitors set your retail pricing, comp checks now and then are good for you. You may actually discover you're way underpriced on some items. This, of course, depends on what market your competitor is in. Being fair to your customers is good. Being fair to yourself is essential.

The Cash Register

The cash register is the most important item in your entire store. This is where the magic happens. Depending on the size of the store, you may need more than one. It's important to have trained, honest, and friendly staff running your registers. The crew members you select must know pot sizes, prices (if a tag is lost), and what classification it goes under. Here are some register rules:

- ✔ Have enough crew trained and ready for the busy season.
- ✔ The registers should be in top shape.
- ✔ Have your crew get your customers through the register quickly. No one likes to wait. If necessary, open another register.
- ✔ Keep impulse items close to the register but never on the counter. Small bags of plant food are a good impulse item.
- ✔ Counters should be clear at all times. No food or drinks at any time. The counter is to conduct business.
- ✔ Have two staff members team together on the register during busy times to keep it moving. One person can scan or enter prices, and one can box items.
- ✔ Have backup staff ready when needed. Have crew available to

cover breaks and days off. Rotate breaks so the register is always covered.

✔ Have a supervisor in charge of registers, supplying register tape and making change.

✔ Someone should be on the register at all times.

The Phone

Besides the register and your sales staff, the telephone is of top importance. Here you don't have that second chance for your first impression. Chances are good that the person on the other end of the phone has never called your store before. Here's what you'll want to practice:

✔ Answer the phone like you just won the lottery. Have excitement in your voice.

✔ Be pleasant and cheery.

✔ Be a good listener.

✔ Ask questions.

✔ Check inventories as needed. Don't assume the computer inventories are right.

✔ Never respond with "I think;" it means you don't know.

✔ Do what you can to get them into the store. Describe the plants they're looking for as "a new crop," "really nice looking right now," or "they are a great price." These, and many other, descriptions are useful to bring them to you.

✔ Thank them for calling. They could have called your competitor.

Special Orders

From time to time your customers will ask you to order something for them. These items may be plants you're currently out of or maybe something you have to search for. There are a few cautions attached to this. First of all, don't bring in a whole truck to accommodate one person's special order. Many of your vendors have minimum order amounts. It's silly to meet this minimum to satisfy one person's needs. If you need enough inventory to justify the order, then fine.

Next, never promise something you may not get. For instance, one of my staff members told a customer that our bedding truck was due on Tuesday. She assured her the begonias she wanted would be on the truck. No problem. Well, there was a problem; my staff member never made me aware of the customer's order. So, the truck showed up without her plants. She was not a happy customer. In fact, she mailed me a long letter complaining about it. Damage control time.

Other times, your customer will want something you get once a year in the spring. For some growers, namely the Bare Root and Balled and Burlap vendors, this is shipping season. Say your customer comes into the store in the fall to order something on one of these spring trucks. They are told the truck will arrive mid-February. So, the customer waits. February rolls around and the truck shows up. One problem. Your customer needed five of a certain plant, but you were sent only three. Your acknowledgement from this company indicated you would be getting five. Where did this go wrong? You call your supplier to find out what happened. You're told they oversold them, and "You were lucky to get the three." If this was supposed to make you feel special that you got three, it didn't. You now get to tell your customer, who, by the way, has five holes already dug, that you won't be able to supply them. Even though the plants were acknowledged and confirmed, stuff happens. The bad part of this situation is that you won't be seeing this truck again until next year. Lesson here: Never promise anything and expect the unexpected. We try our best as salespeople to please everyone. That's our job. But in some cases, things are out of our control. One final note: It's a good idea to get money down from your customer for things you don't usually order or for large quantities. The usual practice is twenty percent down.

Returns and Guarantees

My mentor told me that "the best tomato is the one you sell twice." I've carried this line with me for decades. I've felt it was amusing and truthful. But when you stop and think about it, this may be funny to you, but not for your customer. The simple truth is that the plant you sold them died. Granted it was most likely a weather-related issue, but the result is the same outcome. Your customers come to you for healthy plants and may become discouraged when they fail. This will no doubt happen to you and your staff from time to time. Being understanding is the best position to take. Most of your customers will understand weather-related issues are out of your control. However, some may not. In many cases you're selling your customers a goldfish in a baggie with no instructions on how to care for it. There's no difference really. You can only hope your customer will know how to take care of this living thing. The first step to explaining why the plant met its demise is being understanding. Be sympathetic and never accuse. Educate your customer about what could have gone wrong. Oftentimes the education is enough to have them try again. Explaining proper planting, watering, and feeding are all parts of the educating process.

Oftentimes your customers will appreciate your time and the education, then they buy another one. Other times you're met with resistance. Simply offer a replacement or you can suggest meeting your customer's purchase halfway. This usually takes care of the situation and you've got your cost back in the replacement. The repercussions of a potentially volatile situation are not worth it. Word travels fast if you won't stand behind your products. You don't want a return to ruin any future purchases. It's simply not worth it. Besides, research has found returns and replacements are at less than one percent.

Everyone accepts returns. The grocery store will replace your steak if you didn't like it. Let the public know you stand behind your inventory. Your customer's confidence is important. It's a good idea to have signs posted around your nursery reinforcing your plant guarantee. Remember this rule in retail: You can't please everyone, but you have to try.

Kids

You'll need to teach your staff about when children visit your nursery. This is a great opportunity for teaching and putting the parents' minds at ease. Kids view your nursery as a field trip to the park (a park without swings, anyway). Kids are potentially your future customers. You'll want to make their trip pleasant and memorable.

Parents, of course, are your current customers, so you need to assist them too. It's a bit of a multitasking challenge. You need to take care of your customers and engage their children. Every situation is different, of course. Some parents will have their kids busy doing something to stay entertained.. Still, I feel it's important to engage them. Remember, they're your future customers. The opportunity is too great to pass up. Start simply by saying hello. Maybe then, ask what their name is. This is your hook to engagement. Kids are usually hungry so you may offer a reasonably healthy snack, such as a granola bar, after getting the "okay" from the parents. This may buy you some time to focus on the parents. While continuing through the nursery, point out interesting things such as the fuzzy leaves of Stachys, the snapping snapdragon, or the favorite dragon's blood sedum. Kids love this stuff.

There are safety issues that will come into play at some point:

- running around the nursery
- riding in carts
- toppling birdbaths
- falling into water features
- running in front of traffic

Tie-In Sales

Selling your customer an additional product besides the one they're buying is critical to your business. In fact, it will benefit your customers as well. Here are some ideas that should be useful to your crew as far as tie-in sales are concerned:

Bedding plants

Suggest:

- planting mix
- slow-release fertilizer
- water-soluble fertilizer
- root stimulator
- gloves
- trowel
- watering can
- pottery

Shrubs

Suggest:

- planting mix
- slow-release fertilizer

- ✔ root stimulator
- ✔ gloves
- ✔ shovel

Trees

Suggest:
- ✔ planting mix
- ✔ slow-release fertilizer
- ✔ root stimulator
- ✔ gloves
- ✔ shovel
- ✔ stake
- ✔ tie tape

These are just a few of the tie-in sales you can create.

Christmas

The question you'll need to ask yourself is: "Do I want to convert my nursery into a winter wonderland?" What this will entail is moving, or removing, much of your inventory to make room for Christmas. Every nursery is different. Some will convert the inside of the store. Other nurseries will transform the outside. Any of this takes time and money. Christmas is always a gamble for garden centers. If you have a niche, you have a better chance. Otherwise, you're competing with all the other gift stores, holiday bazaars, and Christmas tree lots that pop up. Remember, the Christmas retail market has a relatively short sales window too. If you have a niche, extra money for Christmas inventory, and advertise heavily, you can succeed. Here are some necessities you'll need to consider:

- ✔ Christmas trees: living, cut, or flocked.

- ✔ Wreaths, greens, swags, and arrangements.

- ✔ Poinsettias are sold just about everywhere. You'll have to run your heaters around the clock. I'd recommend colored ones; they're more unusual.

✔ Giftware: Customers will appreciate a good choice of gifts for the gardener. Unique and unusual garden tools, and garden-related giftware, is a good fit for your store. Try to limit your Christmas stuff to things you feel confident that no one else in your area is selling.

✔ Christmas lights and ornaments are just about everywhere. Be aware and careful in this department. Again, garden-related ornaments are unique enough to sell. The lights are not.

Open House

You'll want to have an open house to attract the public. You'll need to have everything priced and on display. I've found the first weekend in December is the best time for this. You'll have to advertise heavily for this event. Your nursery will be competing for attention with all the various holiday bazaars and local events. This is why advertising is a must. Other Christmas items to note are:

✔ Provide coffee, apple cider, and cookies.

✔ Have holiday music.

✔ Consider door prizes.

✔ Consider a raffle.

✔ Pictures with Santa?

Some last notes to keep in mind: When the holiday season is over, you'll have to take it all down and have a place to store unsold inventory until the next year. You'll have to keep, or get, holiday staff for the season.

The holiday season is fast and furious. Somewhat like the spring, but quicker. Many garden centers do very well during the holiday season. There is a rather large outlay of money to be successful with Christmas. Some nurseries just dabble with it as a way to have winter sales. Others really capitalize on the season. One last note: Have a good supply of gift certificates ready. You'll sell lots of these. Many gardeners will love a gift card from your store for spring purchases.

Some Last Thoughts

✔ As previously mentioned in the Chemicals chapter, have in-house sale contests between staff members to see who can sell the most of a certain product. Offer a prize of your choice to the winner.

✔ Unusual items create interest. Display them well.

✔ Some customers like when you make decisions for them.

✔ Have sales pep talks from time to time.

✔ If you do your job, everyone will leave with something. This is the salesperson's goal.

✔ If you are honored with the "Best of" award, display it proudly. Mention it in your advertising.

✔ Always wear your smile.

Merchandising

THE FIRST RULE TO REMEMBER is that over eighty percent of your customers visit your store as a hobby, the other twenty percent out of necessity. Your customers want to feel happy and motivated during their shopping experience. It's actually a form of stress reduction for many. This is especially true for folks with high-stress jobs. Your customers want to walk into excitement. Don't let them down. You should always have fresh displays that are changed constantly. Again, you never get that second chance to make the first impression.

Displays

Nothing says "buy me" like a big display of color. The buying public loves to see benches full of color. This draws them like a magnet and offers lots of choices. And, of course, your customers always like choices. A large display of color is exactly what you want to establish throughout the spring and summer. These are instant impulse displays. Your endcap displays should be stunning. Hand-picked items are all that should be in these displays. Keep them interesting at all times. You'll want to change these displays often. Keep them fresh. Always use one gallon and larger plants. A display of four-inch color is okay to use as long as you don't mix four inch with other sizes. Smaller plants tend to get lost in displays and are often missed with the hose. Seasonal themes are great to have in displays. Themes are especially effective in endcaps. Holidays and local events are good ideas. You may consider incorporating fertilizers, garden art, statuary pieces, and the like into your displays. Be aware that fertilizer labels may fade in the sun. And, of course, always use waterproof labels with your plant displays.

Plant Blocks Verus Parklike

It's true that plants mixed together make very showy displays. This, versus keeping plants in their groups (blocks), has been a long-time debate with nursery owners. Here's what the discussion is about: If you keep your shrubs in groups, ordering is certainly easier. You can tell at a glance how many have sold. This certainly makes reordering easier. Signing is easier, and so is general maintenance. If a customer calls and needs fifteen Viburnum davidii, you can answer the question with little trouble. You send a staff member out to count and report back. All this seems like the way it should be and has been in many garden centers for years—generations really. The other side of this argument (if you will) is the idea of plants being mixed with other plants, making a parklike, and effective, display. Plants that have been mixed together to show heights, colors, contrasts etc. make a really nice display. Some would suggest this helps to sell more plants. This is where the conversation begins. Does it really? The arrangement certainly looks much more attractive than plants in blocks. But you can't keep track of where all the plants are. Signing is nonexistent and reordering is a nightmare.

Here's a story. Mr. Brown wants ten Sarcococca, but you can only locate seven. Mr. Brown needs ten and leaves to find them at another nursery. You lost the sale. Worse, after he leaves you find another three. This is further compounded by the fact that he had called ahead and was told the computer showed you had ten. This happens. It's really anyone's guess as to which method is best for sales, signing, inventories, and ordering. I've personally worked at garden centers that have done it both ways. Both work. I've taken on a hybrid idea of sorts. I keep my shrubs in blocks and my seasonal gallons in mixed displays. This way customers get the wow factor of the color display and shrubs are easier to locate.

Studying Others

Studying how others put together displays is a good practice. This comes from visiting other garden centers, display gardens at the botanical gardens, etc. In order to keep your displays looking new and exciting, you need ideas. Sure, you're great at what you do, but you would like some fresh ideas. Sometimes this inspiration comes from within your staff. Your crew, as previously mentioned, thinks outside the box. They see things differently. And for this you should be grateful, and work with it. They are going to have ideas you never thought of. As long as you give the indication of what you're trying to create, giving crew members free reign to develop displays is good for them and ultimately good for you and the shop. Be sure to give praise and show appreciation even if it's not exactly what you had in mind. Visiting garden centers both inside and outside of your immediate area is really helpful for display inspiration. Their staff has grouped together the same inventory as you (most likely) in very different fashions. This helps you develop new ideas and will help you with future displays. I would suggest taking a nursery tour several times a year to gather ideas and inspiration. I usually visit four to five outside of my area. It's really surprising how much this helps. You may take a crew member with you. Remember, they see things you don't.

Diversify

As we've talked about, the nursery business is always about change. In order to stay current and exciting to your customers you need to be constantly mixing things up, moving displays around, and adding new merchandise. Your customers will love this. In fact, it helps set you apart from so many other garden centers that don't want, or don't understand why, to keep changing. Here are a few perfect tie-ins to help keep your business ahead of the others:

- garden giftware
- statuary
- nursery-related tools
- pottery
- rare and unusual plants

- bonsai plants and supplies
- pond supplies
- houseplants
- fresh fruit and vegetables
- garden books
- basic hardware
- wooden planters, trellises, etc.
- wall blocks, stepping stones, pavers, etc.
- bulk products; bark, rock, soils, etc.
- snacks

As with anything, it takes money to make money. This we are constantly aware of. It's a good idea to scout the competitors on this one. See what others are trying. Don't just join in. Be different. Try something new. Some of these ideas have a relatively small investment to bring into your nursery. Others will take more. Don't bite off more than you can financially handle. Remember, some of these diversifying programs will take additional staffing too.

Raffle

What an easy way to make money. Every month you set up a fountain at your store right in a centrally located spot. Maybe just inside the building. You want every customer to see it. Then you sell raffle tickets for it. Your customers will love the idea of possibly winning such a great prize for the small price of a ticket. You run this promotion for a month. Charge three to five dollars a ticket. Maybe do a four-for-ten or three-for-ten dollars discount depending on what you charge. At the end of the month a lucky customer wins the fountain. But who really wins is you. You've made enough money on the sale of the lottery tickets to have paid for the fountain as much as ten to twenty times over! Your customers will love the raffle and so will your return on investment. Be sure to have good signing to promote the raffle. Always have the retail price on your sign. Keep at it. Do it once a month, at least, through your twelve golden weeks.

Reducing Inventory

As plants begin to lose their charm, it's time to move them along. This is especially true for annuals. Fertilizing will certainly extend your blooming time and the plants' shelf life. But the time comes to mark it down or write it off and throw it away. Say you have several flats of marigolds that have finished their final bloom cycle in a pot. As long as the plants still look healthy, they're still salable. If they look marginal, dump them. You can reduce them to a fair price for about two weeks, no longer. Remember, the better the deal, the faster they're likely to sell. Quality first; you need to feel good about everything you sell.

You may also consider a midseason clearance on bedding if you've had a slow spring. This will help reduce bedding while the interest is still there. This happens when the weather hasn't been good enough for your fair season customers to buy bedding. It's always a good idea to monitor sales all through the season so you won't be overstocked to begin with. Don't wait until late June to have a bedding sale. By then it's too late to get much interest. Roses and fruit trees are two groups you want to run out of during the season. In other words, these may be best not wintered over. Be cautious with overbuying as always.

Next Year's Purchases

When purchasing for next year you'll want to keep a few things in mind. First, you'll have to commit early (mid-July) to certain plants that are popular and in short supply. In other words, you may still have a good inventory of certain items by midsummer, but growers will want to know what you want for the next year while you're still full. This is just the way it goes. Don't wait until the end of the year to get your orders in, or you're sure to be shorted and disappointed. Roses, berries, fruit trees, etc. will sell out fast at your vendor. You may end up going without them for a year, or more.

Once you've got a few years under your belt it gets easier to anticipate your inventory needs for the following year. Granted, popularity of certain items may vary from year to year. But some items can be counted on for the sake of popularity. Depending on where you live too. Most often roses, fruit trees, berries, and dogwoods will be in big demand and short supply. Ordering early is best. If your garden center is in an area where you sell Bare Root and Balled and Burlap stock, these will surely sell out early. As with anything you sell, keep a close watch as things sell to anticipate your buying needs for the upcoming year. Remember any special orders you may have had that would change your purchasing numbers.

Indoor Shelving

The type of indoor shelving you select will determine the look inside your store, traffic flow, and merchandising options. First of all, you'll need options. The tier-type gondola shelves work best for displaying most of your chemicals, fertilizers, and other products. The shelves adjust, allowing many options for your inventory. These are easy and effective. These can be found in many places. You can research local stores that are going out of business to purchase their shelving. That's what I did. It was a fraction of the price the shelving would have been new.

Shelving manufacturers and distributors can be found online if need be. Be prepared to spend a bit for new shelving. These should be located and priced before submitting your bank loan paperwork. When setting your shelving with product, keep a few things in mind. Smaller bottles (eight ounce/pints) should be on the top tier. Larger bottles and bagged goods should follow below. You'll want to make an effort to keep like-type controls together. Pesticides, fungicides, and herbicides will be best if kept in their respective categories. This makes it easier for your customers and for you as far as reordering goes. It's a good idea to add signing to your displays. Some will come from the company; some you make yourself. Always price every item. Don't leave it to one price tag on the display shelf. These get lost or may end up in front of another item. Customers don't like surprises when it comes to money. Everyone wants to know what price they're paying.

As previously mentioned, big displays of certain types of products are useful and effective. Pallets filled with lawn food, for instance, are an attractive grab-and-go product. The simple fact that you have a large supply of one product suggests that you support and otherwise recommend it. You'll want to display the items you're promoting by season. And don't overdo it. This makes your place look sloppy and will slow traffic flow inside the store. Worse, it confuses the customer. You'll want to keep it simple. Just a few large displays where customers can move around. This will also avoid too many potentially unanswered questions. Remember, good signing, perhaps a shelf talker, is a must. Also keep in mind labels close to windows may fade. Hopefully you'll sell through it fast enough to not be a problem.

Plant Rental

From time to time people will want to borrow plants. This can be disastrous. I've tried several approaches to this. These seem to be the best methods I've found. Plants or products used for weddings and noncommercial use are totaled up (excluding tax) then charged a twenty percent usage fee per day.

Example: plant total = $200.00

20% = $40.00

Rental fee = $40.00 per day

This is certainly a fair rate for borrowing. I also limited the rental to three days. I inspected all plants upon return for condition. If plants are damaged, the customer pays the full retail price. This seldom happened, however. This policy is best put into place at the time of the rental. Be sure to mention the following:

1. Plants can't be transported in a truck due to wind damage.

2. Plants are to be watered as soon as they reach their destination.

3. Check the plants' water needs daily.

4. Be careful not to damage plants when loading and unloading or moving from place to place.

5. Don't put shade plants in the sun.

Additional notes: Don't let anyone borrow plants in anything smaller than a one-gallon size pot. Four-inch color dries out too quickly. People renting plants don't usually understand how to care for plants the way nursery staff does. The rental program is used generally to discourage rental at all.

Plants for commercial applications and plants loaned to schools and other community functions may actually help promote your business. This should only be done if your nursery name is mentioned in the function's program or by signage. It's a good idea to have several signs made with your name or logo on them to be loaned out with your plants. A few different signs are best. If you send signing out with the plants, you can be fairly safe in assuming they will be displayed. People are usually too busy setting up the function to create a sign for your benefit. Be sure to explain the necessity of signage when the plants are loaned. This can (and should) be free advertising for your nursery.

A Few Extra Notes

- Price everything!
- Your inventory should be reflected by your sales market and customer base.
- Plan to set your prices to the nearest ninety-ninth cent.
- Don't be intimidated by big box stores. Remember, they're your best advertising. My garden center was half a mile from a big store. It helped us greatly.
- Take advantage of overstock and clearance items from your vendors. Be careful with plants, however; they may be overgrown, out of bloom, or otherwise undesirable.
- If you are scanning prices by bar codes, be aware that some may be damaged or lost on plant material. Have a backup plan.
- Ground plant displays may be useful in displaying a plant as it matures. I'm not convinced that the sales you may get from a displayed item justifies the space taken by the display. I used one for several years and removed it.
- Always create new ideas and ways to expand and increase your business.

Marketing

THERE ARE TWO BASIC STRATEGIES for marketing your garden center. You can sell a lot for a little, or a little for a lot. You really don't want to be known for the latter strategy. It's been said that you can set your pricing based on your target customers' zip code. This is true to a point. However, word travels fast if you're overpriced. Affluent neighborhoods are certainly a good customer base to pull from. However, you'll sell more product if you don't overcharge. Again, word travels fast and besides, everyone likes a deal. Keep your prices fair, and you will do well. Again, when you buy smart, you can sell smart. Don't get into the trap of buying from expensive growers. There are some very overpriced growers out there. Be careful. This rule applies to your hard goods line as well. High-end stuff sells slowly, tying up your money. Again, be smart.

Let's move on to promotion. Promotion is the key to marketing your store. How do you plan on promoting your business? You have to do something. Customers aren't going to just find you. Word of mouth helps. Advertising will help more but you have to have an angle to bring people into your store. More importantly, get them to come back. Here are the essentials:

- ✔ good location
- ✔ quality merchandise

- good prices
- great customer service
- knowledgeable staff
- good selection
- good value for the money
- good sales and promotions
- pleasant shopping experience
- friendly staff
- exciting atmosphere all around

"What does this have to do with promotion?" you ask. Simple, these are all key components to marketing your store. Having things that others don't. Such as any of the above. If you're missing any of the key factors above, you're slipping. Strive to keep these in play at all times. This will keep the buying public coming back to your store. Then, and only then, the word of mouth begins.

Handouts

Having handouts helps market your store by the knowledge created in them. This also helps to promote your inventory. Always recommend products you sell in your handouts. Many nurseries don't take advantage of this easy marketing tool. Customers ask questions because they need help. They've chosen you. As you build your customers' trust, they'll usually buy what you suggest.

Think about it this way. You have a broken water pipe under your sink. You don't know what to do. So, you take the broken part into a specialty shop. The salesperson shows you what you need to fix it. Sold. That's how it works for you too. Below are some examples of handouts you can create to sell product. There are many more, of course. My store had about thirty. Always have your store logo at the top of each handout. It's cheap advertising that may be shared with others too.

- planting a lawn
- monthly lawn care schedule
- flowers for cutting
- creating an herb garden

✔ vegetable growing tips

✔ trees for shade or fall color

✔ fragrant plants

✔ shade plants

✔ attracting butterflies and bees

✔ deer-proof plants

✔ organic controls

✔ flowering plants by season

✔ proper planting of trees and shrubs

✔ plants for hot or dry locations

Make your printouts easy to read. Carefully plan out which will be the most needed in your community. Be sure to restock on a regular basis. Check periodically to be sure you have the inventory of items you suggest. And be sure to introduce your customers to the handout station. After a while they'll be trained to help themselves. This is not only a great way to instruct your customers, but to sell merchandise. And remember, the chances are good that they're going to tell a friend.

Demonstrations and Clinics

In-store demonstrations are good for your community and good for your sales. Plan these out months in advance. Advertise what the topic will be. Most should be free to the public. You may have signups if you don't have much space for the events. You can expect to sell quite a bit of merchandise that relates to your topic. It wasn't unusual for me to sell thirty pairs of clippers when I did a rose pruning seminar. This, in addition to many other related products.

Here's what to expect:

✔ Invite the novice to your store. If you win their trust, they'll be back. Chances are good they'll tell their friends.

✔ Sell merchandise. Always be prepared to have every possible tie-in item on hand that relates to your discussion. Have plenty of backstock too. You will go through it.

✔ Inform your audience. These seminars will grow and build your reputation as the garden expert. The more you, or your staff, perform, the better you are known in your community.

✔ Help to move slow-moving inventory. You'll be able to move some of those slow-moving plants as long as you promote them. If you propagate some plants, and suggest them, this is great profit for you.

✔ Be sure to have a knowledgeable staff member, or yourself, conduct these classes. The last thing you want is to have an uninformed staff member fumble their way through it. There will be plenty of questions from your audience.

✔ Conduct out of the main business area. It's best to have an area set up for your clinics that's not in the immediate area of your sales areas. This keeps the whole setting like a classroom setting. It also prevents others from joining, especially if a fee is taken. It's best to have a cover over this area for sun and rain protection.

✔ Chart your success. It's a good idea to keep notes on each event. This will help you track attendees, shortcomings of inventory, and hits and misses of topics. Plan to offer several topics a month if you're able to manage it. Your community will really appreciate the classes. Meantime, you're building trust and selling products.

Who You're Up Against
~ Big Box (well sort of)

As I've mentioned previously, most of the people that shop at big boxes are not your customers. However, since they sell plants, they do take away from your sales. Here's what they're about:

✔ grab-and-go sales approach

✔ no sales help

✔ no carryout trays

✔ no knowledge

✔ on your own

✔ limited selection

✔ questionable quality

✔ displays not attended to

✔ not as inexpensive as once thought

✔ Most color displays are guaranteed sales. What doesn't sell, gets replaced by the grower.

✔ If you can replace just one of these strategies, you're on the right track. The goal is to address them all.

~ Supermarkets

The supermarket approach is to entice the seasonal shopper with color. Again, these are seldom your customers. But they sell plants, nonetheless. This takes away from your sales.

✔ grab-and-go approach, again

✔ color only

✔ no shrubs etc.

✔ no knowledge

✔ on your own

✔ most items in bad shape

✔ watered only as needed, maybe

✔ have to shop before entering the store

Again, as you can see these shouldn't be considered your competitors. In fact, they're really (or should be) considered your best advertising. Work on these weaknesses.

~ Buying Online

How many times have you looked up the description of a plant only to be taken to a plant vendor? Sure, you'll get the description alright, but have you paid attention to the offerings? Crazy really. You can buy a shrub or tree from your store for a fraction of the price they're asking through online vendors. This makes a person wonder if people fall for this overinflated madness. One also has to wonder if potential (online) shoppers just assume all plants, everywhere, are expensive. Your job again is to constantly be aware of the four main rules: quality, service, selection, and value. In this case the value part of the big four rules is the one you need to impress to your customers. Potentially quality too.

Catalogs

Picture this: It's mid-January. It's nowhere near planting season. The mail arrives and there it is—the glossy, colorful catalog with every flowering plant imaginable. Their marketing approach is a simple one. Display a booklet full of colorful spring plantings. However, the ingenious part of this marketing plan is when the catalog arrives. Mid-January. Most every potential gardener is inside eager for spring planting season. What a great way to get a jump on the season. "If I buy it now, it will be spring." Again, an ingenious marketing approach. We don't need to go into further questioning on the subject of quality, value, etc. This is about marketing. Most of the folks that have purchased from these companies have, or will, become your customers. This is a good thing.

The In-Store Coffee Shop

What better way to market your garden center than to have a coffee shop on-site. It sounds good, but is it? Really seems like a perfect fit. Picture this: A husband and wife want to beat the crowd to your store on a busy Saturday. They don't have time to stop for coffee, but it's at your place. Or a mom and her daughter want to walk through your place to pick out shrubs for the daughter's new yard. "Hey, let's stop in for a coffee." What's so bad about either of these scenarios? Well, maybe nothing. Seems like a good idea. But, as with anything, there are risks involved. Here are some considerations:

- It is really a separate business venture.
- Will your local zoning allow you to have a coffee shop? The zoning in my town wouldn't allow a coffee shop. Be aware.
- The permitting process may be lengthy.
- You need knowledgeable staff members for making coffee.
- Staffing for the shop. You'll need someone to run this venture

while your store is open.

✔ Initial outlay. Again, this is a separate business venture that will take quite a bit of money for start-up costs. Not to mention constant inventory costs.

✔ Seating. It's probably a good idea to have an area for customers to sit while enjoying their coffee. This may encroach on your sales area.

Some Final Notes

✔ Promote your business every way you can.

✔ Have a sale for every possible occasion.

✔ Consider a spring kickoff event—free tomatoes for the first 100 customers, door prizes, raffle, etc. Be creative.

✔ Advertise "Grower direct" if it applies. This sends a message that you have fresh and affordable inventory.

✔ Remember, you're not just marketing your store, you're marketing yourself. Always be a step ahead.

Signing

INFORMATIONAL SIGNING is very helpful in the nursery business. Most people don't know about plants like you do. The public wants and needs to be taught about what you sell. In fact, signing is like having a plastic salesperson explaining about the plant. You would be surprised just how many garden centers don't do informational signs at all! They're missing out on a ton of sales. This practice will greatly promote your plant sales. In fact, it will set you apart from your competition who, most likely, won't do it. It does take time to create these signs, but it really pays off.

Informational Signs

The signs you create to help sell your plants should be around five-by-seven inches and be blank white. Always use fade resistant, UV-rated black ink. These are special markers you can find at office supply stores. Permanent markers will fade. Always use good handwriting. If your handwriting isn't the best, have a crew member write them for you. You'll most likely have to put the information on paper for them first. When the signs are finished you can simply staple them on to a two-foot piece of lathe wood (one-half by two). It helps to cut one edge at an angle to easily push into the potted plant. A power saw works well for this.

The information you use on the signs should be simple, inviting, and use high points. Though professional plant people talk in botanical names, you may want to stick to common names when making signs. The sign should include the following:

- ✔ name
- ✔ height
- ✔ bloom color and time
- ✔ evergreen or deciduous
- ✔ sun or shade
- ✔ misc. high points:
- ✔ fragrant
- ✔ deer-proof
- ✔ drought tolerant
- ✔ long blooming

The more you highlight the plant, the more attractive it looks to your customer. An additional note: Most plant people will use the height a plant will attain in a ten-year period as the height on the sign. You should do a weekly walk through for damaged signs. Replace them as needed. Though it's a job, new signs should be made every year. This is a good winter project. Informational signs are primarily used on trees and shrubs.

Directional Signs

Directional signs are used to highlight certain areas. These signs are larger so they will stand out from a distance. These signs are usually anywhere from one- to two-foot tall (or more) to two- to four-feet wide (or more). These should have large, solid, block-type lettering. These should be professionally made on a polycarbonate-type backing. Depending on climate, these signs should last many years. Some directional signs may include:

- ✔ berries
- ✔ flowering trees
- ✔ shade trees
- ✔ fruit trees

- ✔ hedging shrubs
- ✔ dwarf conifers
- ✔ broadleaf evergreens
- ✔ shade plants
- ✔ herbs
- ✔ perennials
- ✔ vines
- ✔ water gardens
- ✔ bonsai
- ✔ potting soils
- ✔ planters
- ✔ vegetables
- ✔ grasses

This, of course, will change from nursery to nursery.

Bedding Tables

Since bedding plants will, most likely, be your biggest draw, signing is essential. A bench containing Traypaks or four-inch color should have a price sign at least every five feet. Bedding signs can be more colorful than your directional yard signs. In fact if you have a talented artistic-type crew member on board, you can make colorful and creative signs. Use color markers with permanent (UV if possible) ink. The signs should have some information about the plants, besides just being colorful. The five-by-seven size placard works well for this. However, eight-by-ten size can certainly allow for more graphic design, wording, and pricing.

Individual Price Tags

With the exception of Traypaks and four-inch color spots, everything should have an identifiable price tag on it. A five-inch stick-type tag displays the price perfectly on four-inch perennials and one-gallon pots. A wraparound-type price tag is best for anything larger than a one-gallon size pot. These are especially useful for trees and large shrubs. They show up well for your customers to see. Be sure to use a UV-rated pen when making tags. You don't want the price to fade over the year. Price tags will need to be replaced each year due to the plastic becoming brittle.

A custom printed price tag is nice and easy to use. Custom tags are available through specialty tag companies. An additional note: Since plants are moved around quite frequently, tags may get lost in the shuffle. It's a good idea to have a crew member do a walk through every so often to replace lost or damaged tags. If you have each staff member be in charge of an area in your nursery, this is quite easily done.

Pricing Soil Bags

I've seen many ideas through the years with regard to pricing soil bags. Some garden centers have a three-ring binder with pictures and prices. Some have a floating sign (placard stapled to a block of wood) with the price on it. Others assume you know what you want and look it up in a computer. Still others have no price showing at all. This leaves the customer to guess the price. None of these are really tried and true methods for pricing your bagged soils. What seemed to work well with my store was this: I displayed an empty bag of each bagged soil on the wall above and behind the counter. You simply staple the bag to the wall and attach a price to each bag represented. I got this idea from one of the many fast-food restaurants. Works for them, worked for me.

Some Extra Thoughts

Lots of wholesale nurseries are offering priced tags on their plants (at a cost). My thought is that the price you pay for the label is worth the money. All you have to do when the delivery truck shows is simply check in the order and put it away. This convenience is great during the busy season. Just think how long it would take your staff to price everything. Sometimes your crew gets called away while tagging and may not finish until the next day. Simply said, you're losing sales. One additional note: You do have to check the price tags before putting the plants away. Mistakes happen. I once had a $2.99 price tag marked as $22.99. Just pay attention.

Adhesive pricing labels attached to the pot are becoming popular. Some will have a brief description and growing conditions of the plant. These are very useful. The only drawback is that the label on the pot is where you find the price. This may be a bit challenging for the customer. It does help in a pinch, but additional pricing is helpful, preferably above (or attached to) the plant.

Always promote a new item with a sign that says "new." Don't be afraid to charge a bit more too.

Remember, good signing means more sales and happier customers.

Advertising

ADVERTISING IS ESSENTIAL. To have a business without advertising is really not an option. Think about it: How else will your potential customer know about you and your business? If you are just starting into business, there's all the more need to get your name known. Your community is all about change. People come, people go. It's the parade factor. You have to be aware of this and advertise, advertise, advertise. You have to promote yourself and your business as the gardening experts. Yours should be the name people think of when they think of plants. You'll have to convince your potential customers of this every time you advertise. Building trust through your approach is paramount.

The Guts of Your Ads

The frequency in which you advertise says something, if not everything, about your garden center. You need to get, and keep, yourself in front of your buying public. By being consistent, people will be expecting to hear from you as your business grows. Keep your ads to the season you're currently in so people can relate to you. Be creative. The more creative you are the more you'll be noticed. Get your customers' attention with any ad you create. Gardeners crave your information and wisdom. Teach and sell in every ad. Teaching will get you noticed. It will also help you become the local expert status you want, and deserve, for yourself and your garden center.

This doesn't come overnight; stay at it. No negative messages or slamming the competition. That's not what you, or the business, are about. Focus on the positive. Boast about your selection. Quality and new items. Talk about what sets you apart from everyone else. "Stop by and see what all the buzz is about." Let your customers know what makes your nursery different and better than any of the others. Boasting is okay to do. Think about where you've come from and think about where you want your nursery to go. You sell quality; let everyone know that. Also, it's best not to mention prices in any of your ads. The exception would be printed media, such as the newspaper. But keep it simple; not a bunch of priced items, just a few. It's best to price only items you know will make a statement. But again, your customers would prefer to see your ads contain information. Information and mentioning products will be a sure way to get them into your store. Once you've got them to your store, you have the possibility of selling even more. Again, your wisdom will get them back to your store. Target your ads at "you" not "I" or "me." It's more personal. Also plan on using half of your year's advertising budget during your twelve golden weeks of spring. You've got fish on the line, now reel them in.

The Reader Board

Regardless of what signing you have at the street, it's direct advertising for you. You'll want to use this wisely and with the right message. Be short with what you want to say. People driving by at a certain speed can't, and won't, read it. Simple is always best. Three to four words tops. Less is more in this case. Again, unless it's a featured item, try to refrain from advertising a price. You want the interest in the sign to get people into your store. Try to avoid words such as "are here" or "in stock;" that's obvious and takes up space on your sign. Use your sign to sell something. Pansies, fragrant daphne, blooming heather. You get the idea. This is some of, if not your only, free advertising. Sure, it's limited to your drive-by traffic. But it's nonetheless an effective, and useful, tool for promotion. You'll want to change your street reader every week. People will stop looking at your sign if it stays the same for any longer. Keep it short, keep it simple, and sell something.

The Monthly Handout

Every nursery should create a monthly gardening handout. This should be kept at the front counter in front of the register or POS station. This makes it easy for your customers to pick one up while they're waiting for their order to be processed. As mentioned, these need to be changed out every month. This is your chance to let your customers know what they should be doing in the garden during the month. This is a great way to teach your customers about what you know about gardening. It's also a great way to build your reputation as the garden expert. But there's more. In these monthly newsletters you can also sell product. And you should. Your customers want and need to be told what to do, and when. Seasonal feedings, fungicide, pesticide, and herbicide usage can all be explained and promoted here. It's a great way to educate, build your image, and sell product. Your customers will appreciate the newsletter. They won't even pay attention to the sales angle.

The Media

Some time ago my daughter was working with me at the nursery. She said, "Watch this," and ran a "one hour only" special sale and posted it online. The parking lot was full in minutes! Wow, a superior advertising medium is born. I'd been raised with newspaper, radio, and TV ads. In fact I remember when the nursery with the largest ad in the yellow page was the winner. But this to me was very different. It was direct and got results immediately. Here's the breakdown:

Internet

The bottom line in advertising is when you advertise online, many people will see you. Great exposure for sure. If you create a web page to promote your business, you'll get lots of attention. People, gardeners, and maybe future gardeners will all be exposed to your business. It takes a bit of work to create a web page, but it's worth it. What better way to display your business to the public all day and night? You can introduce new items, run promotions, and show pictures of anything. It's a great marketing tool for your business.

Radio

Radio is broadcast inside many businesses, cars, and homes. It's a great means of promoting your business. Your message, though short, is direct to the audience your radio format customer has chosen. You have to be selective when choosing a station. You want to be on the station that best suits your customer base. You can stir excitement with your enthusiasm and should. You can further your customers' education by giving gardening tips. This is especially valuable. Not only are you driving home the point that you're the local expert, but you're also selling a product of your choice. Some of your vendors will offer co-op money to help you pay for your advertising. This helps a lot. Another expense that's worth buying is a jingle. A professional outfit will put this together for you. It's a bit of a cost but you'll be glad you did. It's played at the intro to your ad. My customers would come into my nursery whistling or singing it. A great hook for your garden center.

Newspaper

Actual newsprint isn't around nearly as much as it used to be. However, many of your customers still read the paper. Writing a weekly garden column is what I did as part of my advertising. My customers would cut the ad out, bring it into the nursery, and say, "Sell me all the things you said I need in your ad." This happened quite frequently. That alone made running the ad worthwhile. The other part of this is that, again, you're establishing yourself as the local garden expert. Co-op money can be available for this as well to offset the costs. Many newspapers are online now.

Television

If you're in a large market, TV may be for you. It's expensive. Reaches only the audience that's watching the channel. With so many channels to watch, it's hit and miss at best. Your best bet is to do a gardening show on a local station. The costs are minimal. You're hitting a local customer base and you're more apt to get a better response.

Billboard

A good idea for your business. I had one for my business. You'll want to be sure you select a busy route within your market zone. People read billboards. Again, it's getting, and keeping, your business name out there. Like your reader board, you'll want to keep it simple. Your business name, logo (maybe) and one tagline. Something easy to read like Your Gardening Experts works well. Remember, the folks that will see your sign are traveling fast. Too fast to read much wording. One additional note: Make it stand out with color.

Direct Mail

I've done direct mail for many years. Here's my take on it. First, you'll have to pick a target zip code you feel best alerts your potential customer. This can be expensive depending on populations within the area. You may feel more than one zip code would be best. It's a gamble to reach your potential customer and more cost to you. Second, you'll need to have a gimmick to be noticed and get the customer to visit your store. The idea of selling yourself as the garden expert doesn't work here. It simply doesn't catch the attention you'll need to attract your customer or pay for the mailing. Incidentally, co-op advertising monies may be available from your vendors to help offset the cost. Lastly, as mentioned, you'll need a gimmick. My nursery gave away a free tomato plant. This caught attention. It was a cost to the nursery nonetheless. Is all this worth it you ask? It's certainly a gamble like any advertising. Are you going to get the response you're looking for with direct mail? You have a good possibility of bringing in the customer that has never been to your store. This by itself is a win.

Coupons

The idea behind the coupon is to reward your current customer. Unless you produce a coupon in a mailer, that's what you'll get. Depending on your angle, this might be a good way to thank your customers for their patronage. It may also be a way to have your customers spend more. An example would be: spend $200.00 and we'll take twenty percent off. So your customer tries to get their purchases to $200.00 to use the coupon. This works for a while. But, like any coupon deal there are some downfalls. The biggest problem arises when a frequent customer tells you that they forgot their coupon at home. This is a really uncomfortable position to be in. What do you do? Do you stand by your store policy of having to present the coupon at the time of the sale? This is naturally upsetting to your customer. You may lose them as a customer. And again word travels fast. Or do you honor the coupon left at home and make an exception? If you do this, you run the risk of either your customer doing it again or a customer overhearing the conversation and trying it then or at a later date. This happened repeatedly at my store. It's an uncomfortable position to be in. Therefore, I would shy away from this promotion.

Extra Ad Stuff

There is a world of things you can put your name on. You have to be careful not to get carried away. It's really easy to. I've found the best items to have my name put on are the following:

- baseball caps
- pens
- coffee mugs
- keychains
- T-shirts

These are the top five items that had the best customer response through the years I was in business. Oh yes—don't forget business cards.

Final Advertising Notes

People won't respond to promotions or sales for anything less than twenty percent off.

With any promotion, the goal is to get your potential customer into your store. More importantly, to have them come back again.

Tracking your advertising success is nearly impossible. An idea that worked for me was to have a clipboard near the register. The questionnaire on the clipboard was titled "How did you hear about us?" This gave me at least an idea where my advertising money was working.

The Weather

OUR INDUSTRY IS CONSIDERED A FAIR SEASON ONE. In other words, customers visit when the weather is good. Snow, rain, heatwave, you might as well be closed. Besides the obvious, the weather is important to the nursery person for many reasons. Watching for the last frost date is one of these reasons. Your customers have to be careful when planting tender plants such as annuals and many vegetables. If planted too early in the spring, these crops will suffer or perish. Not only is the air too cold, the soil is too. Close attention must be paid by you when ordering tender items. Be prepared to keep this tender stock under cover until the frost has passed. When selling these crops early, be sure to have some signs warning your customer of cold damage. You'll always want to buy when the weather forecast is for good weather. This being said, don't fill your bedding benches if rain is in the forecast for a week. You're relatively safe if it's only raining for a few days. No longer. You're tying up your money. Besides, sales will be slow. You won't be moving much inventory. If your bedding area is covered, go ahead with your purchases. However, your sales will still be slow. Buy with caution. An additional note about the rain: Water can greatly reduce the color on your bedding plants. The plants will have to be cleaned to be salable again.

The wind is an important weather consideration to know about. Wind dries out plants, trees, shrubs, bedding, all of it. Wind is especially hard on bedding plants. The pots they arrive in hold very little soil. The soil dries out quickly on a windy day. Rewatering is necessary. Also, wind can damage tender young seedlings. This is especially true for plants that haven't been hardened off. Protect by sheltering during windy conditions. Misting is helpful to reduce moisture loss. Wind-damaged bedding plants may be permanently damaged. Trees and shrubs can be targets to wind damage too. Newly forming growth can be wind burned. Misting with the hose will help this. Plants that are rootbound, or otherwise stressed in their pots, will always be in need of additional watering. This is certainly an area to keep your eyes on. The sun can damage plants in many ways as well. First, you can experience sunburn on leaves when the weather switches quickly from cool to hot. This is usually in the springtime. The newly forming tender growth can become sunburned without much notice. As previously mentioned, plants may need to be watered several times during hot days. The least amount of stress on plants, the better.

Landscape Design

A LANDSCAPE DESIGN SERVICE CAN DO WONDERS to increase your bottom line. Of course, this takes a strong knowledge of plant material in your climate zone and a good eye for designing. Your customers will be unaware that you provide this service. Once again advertising and promoting this service is a must. Your overstock and slow-moving inventories are great to figure into your designs. Propagated plant material is even better to add. This service will catch on after you've done it for a while. You'll find customers will search you out for your service. Word of mouth will come in handy for referrals too. All said, it's a great way to make money. Especially during the quiet months. Be fair with your design price and you should expect a good addition to your business. By securing a good, reliable landscaper to install your designs you'll be even stronger. If you decide to have a landscape business of your own, you'll be starting an additional business. Keep this in mind. You most likely won't be able to pull from your crew for this. I've seen this happen. It doesn't usually end well. Be aware and be careful. Here is basic designing in a nutshell:

1. **Measure the property and/or beds.**
2. **Create a diagram on paper of the plot.**

    ✔ Show the house, walkways, trees, buildings, and existing landscape.

✔ Show any lay of land changes (slopes, grades).

✔ Show power lines above and below ground.

✔ Show which direction is south.

3. Break design into three basic sections.

✔ Public garden, front yard.

✔ Living or private area, backyard.

✔ Service area, shed, storage, trash area, etc.

4. Study other landscapes in the area.

✔ Decide if you want formal or informal balance.

✔ Develop specialty plots for cut flowers, herbs, etc., if desired.

✔ Try to landscape for the lowest amount of maintenance.

✔ Mix evergreen with deciduous material for the best effect.

✔ Consider different bloom times with your choices.

✔ Use leaves for texture and color contrast.

5. Study the structure of the house.

✔ Understand the house contour (peaks, etc.).

✔ Understand ultimate plant heights, cleanliness, etc.

✔ Don't over- or underplant.

✔ Smaller plants for a smaller home, larger plants for a larger home.

✔ Use plants to frame in the structure, balance, and compliment.

✔ Use trees to give the illusion of space.

6. More yard, less maintenance.

✔ Avoid sharp corners (speeds mowing, creates flow).

✔ Leave lawn areas unbroken (saves trimming, creates space.

✔ Apply a bark, or mulch, cover to improve appearance, reduce weeds, and improve moisture-holding qualities.

✔ Select some slower-growing plants. This will shorten maintenance time.

✔ Annuals and perennials are good for color but require more work.

7. Areas of concern:

- covering up potential view spots
- covering especially bad views (neighbors, buildings etc.)
- planting on a slope
- especially wet, dry, or hot spots
- keeping plants that attract bees away from the house or patio areas
- screening plants to block wind
- planting around deer
- sun versus shade planting
- understand plant growth rates
- planting around and under trees

Safety

SAFETY IN YOUR GARDEN CENTER IS PARAMOUNT. You sell heavy inventory, chemicals, and water is everywhere. You have to be always on the lookout for potential hazards at all times. Your customers need, and deserve, to be safe in your store. Here are some general safety items you can expect to encounter:

Carts

What is always a concern is carts tipping over when unloaded improperly. Overloaded carts can tip as well. Carts left in aisles or parking areas are hazards. Children shouldn't ride in carts for their own safety.

Hoses

Tripping over hoses is the main safety issue at garden centers. Pulling hoses while someone is standing on them is always a potential danger too. Staff needs to be shown proper hose usage, placement, and safety concerns. The wand at the end of the hose should never be left in an aisle either. This is a common mistake made by crew members.

Open Aisles

Boxes of items to be restocked should never be left in the aisles. Aisles need to remain clear for easy access by your customers and staff. In the yard, aisles must remain clear as well. Plants should be put back into their blocks after customers have made their choices. Bedding plants need to be off the ground. This is a real hazard for your customers and your staff. If you must, store bedding flats under benches until you can get them processed. You and your crew should always make an attempt to keep aisles clear of flats, carts, and hoses. Keep your shopping customers in mind.

Lifting

You sell heavy inventory. Trees, soils, planters, etc. can cause potential lifting issues. Safe lifting must be practiced by you and the crew. Your staff needs to be on the lookout for customers that may need help lifting. If a customer looks like they may need help, assist them. Besides the safety issues, customer service comes first. Lifting issues are one of the biggest problems in the nursery business.

Loading Vehicles

Care should be taken when loading your customers' vehicles. This becomes easier the more it's done. Some common issues are lifting heavy things into the vehicle. Always get help. Damaging a vehicle is a common garden center problem. Special care must be taken here. Truck beds can be scratched, staked plants should be laid down in vehicles to avoid piercing the headliner. Laying down plants in the passenger seat may cause a visual block for the driver. Be aware. Liquids should always be bagged. Then there's the dirt issue. Since much of your inventory contains dirt, boxes should be used. A plastic trunk liner is also useful.

Tools

Pruning shears are the tool of the trade. Your clippers are usually, or should be, very sharp. Care must be taken when using your clippers. I can't tell you how many times I've cut myself. It's usually either being in a hurry or not paying attention that gets you cut. My advice is to not be in a hurry. Pay attention to what you're pruning. Wearing gloves can be a good idea too.

There have been lots of times I've cut my glove and not my finger. Be careful. Impress this on your staff as well. Share the importance of clipper safety. This should be brought up in your safety meetings. Revisit the issue often. Rakes, shovels, brooms, etc. should always be put away when not in use. It's really easy to leave tools out. This is especially true when we get called away from our task. If you're working with a tool and get called away, simply put your tools out of the aisle. This will stop a potential accident.

Water

Water is the lifeline of our business. This goes without saying. Besides hose safety, there are other concerns. The issue of slipping on a slick surface is one of these hazards. More times than not, this happens when moss or algae is present on the surface. Have the crew be aware of these areas. Treat the areas with the appropriate algicide or moss remover before this becomes a problem. The slipping is also a problem in winter with ice. This is a real hazard for your staff and customers. Certainly be aware of the potential for ice (if your zone freezes) and sprinkle ice melter down as soon as possible.

Kids like to play in water. For whatever reason, it's an attraction. You'll need to be aware of this at all times. Don't let children near ponds at your nursery. The temptation to go in the water is too great. You can't take the chance. If you have a pond at your garden center, you'll have to make it so kids aren't able to get near it. We had one at my nursery. We ended up putting a fence around it at first. After a while we removed it altogether. Bird baths are another safety concern. Kids seem to like splashing the water out of your birdbaths. Again, you'll have to be aware of this. If a bird bath were to fall on a child, it could be a tragedy. Be very careful in how you display these. Either display the top leaning against the base, have no water in them, or completely surround them with plants. These display ideas will limit a young child's attraction to them. Hoses are an attraction with kids too. Just wrap them up when you're done watering. You should anyway. This will slow down, if not stop, the interest.

The last comment about water safety is simple. Drink lots of it. You work outside in the sun (during summer anyway). You need to stay hydrated. It took me years to learn the importance of drinking lots of water. You'll just feel better.

Visits from OSHA

Just when you least expect it, you'll get an unscheduled and unexpected visit from the folks at OSHA (Occupational Safety and Health Administration). This department is set up to help your business run safely. They will require a few hours of one of your staff member's time. This crew member can't be a relative. And they want the meeting to happen as soon as they arrive. A little surprising, but here's what they'll want: They'll interview your staff member about safety concerns. They'll walk around and take pictures of potential problems. They'll want to be sure you're having monthly safety meetings. They'll want to see the notes from these meetings, and the names of all attendees. You'll need to have all of your Safety Data Sheets (SDS) available for each chemical you sell. And, if you don't have a company safety manual, you'll need to create one. So just be aware this inspection is for your business' benefit. However, it can happen at any time. Be ready with everything I've mentioned.

Visits from the Fire Department

Inspections from your local fire department can also happen at any time. These visits are usually once a year. It's helpful to know what they're looking for. For the most part, the safety issues they'll be looking for should be common safety issues you practice already. It's good, however, to have another set of eyes helping you in the safety department. Here is a list of safety issues they'll likely be looking for:

- all building exits clearly marked
- excessive or unsafe use of extension cords
- no blocked isles
- current fire extinguisher dating
- minimum aisle widths
- spill kit for chemicals
- hazardous areas or materials
- sprinkler system (if applicable)
- proper building lighting

It's good to know, and practice, the safety concerns your fire department will be looking for. After their inspection you'll receive a report of their findings. If you are in violation of anything, you'll be given a certain time frame in which to comply. If you just think "safety," you can't go wrong.

Safety Meetings

Your store needs to perform monthly safety meetings. All current employees are to attend these meetings. They'll have to sign the meetings minutes validating their attendance. Here are some topics you may discuss:

- current safety issues
- upcoming safety issues (busy season)
- ways to resolve and prepare for current and upcoming safety issues
- fire extinguisher safety
- hose safety
- tool safety, including pruners
- lifting issues
- spill kit
- aisles
- slipping and falling issues
- electrical safety
- first aid kit
- proper clothing
- employee input

Every garden center comes with their own set of safety issues. Keep on top of safety for your staff and your customers' protection.

More Safety Notes

A few "Ask for help if you need it" signs set around your nursery will help with lifting and sales.

- Always keep an eye on children.
- You and your staff need to be aware of parking lot safety.

- ✔ Poisonous plants should be signed as such.
- ✔ Be aware of the potential eye danger of twiggy plants.
- ✔ Tomato cages should have a plastic pot covering the unprotected legs to protect staff, and customers, from danger.
- ✔ Always think before lifting. If it's heavy, get help.
- ✔ There should be no running in the nursery by anyone.

Greenhouse Notes

MANY GARDEN CENTERS either have a greenhouse or will build one. There are many things to know about greenhouse production. I'm only going to explain the main issues you'll need to be aware of.

Sterile Conditions

Without good sterile conditions in your greenhouse, you can have fungal and bacterial issues. Remember what happens when you leave the bread on the counter too long? Exactly. Don't let this happen in your greenhouse. Fungi problems will spread very quickly. Always clean your greenhouse before you fill it. Spray the appropriate fungicide and cleaner (or bleach and water) on all surfaces, including your benches. Be sure all weeds are gone too.

Air Circulation

Air movement should be at its best. When you walk through the large greenhouses at your growers, you're almost knocked over with the wind. Air movement slows down fungal development and moves the heat around too. Fans need to be running at all times.

Temperature

The heat you'll desire depends on the crops you are growing. This can be all over the place. In general, most houses want to be around sixty-five degrees at the warm end and sixty degrees at the cooler end of the house. Again, this varies with the crops you're raising. Thermometers are a must-have. You'll want to have several. Keep a good watch on them to monitor the warmth at various spots around the house.

Plant Spacing

As plants mature, they need to be spaced. This is especially important in greenhouse growing. This allows good air circulation between each and slows down fungus problems. Equally important is that plants will stretch if not spaced. This is even more of a problem in the greenhouse than on the bedding tables outside. Plants, especially bedding, grow quickly and are prone to stretching if not spaced.

Spraying

Insects, namely whiteflies, aphids, and mites, are common in the greenhouse climate. Diseases too. The enclosed area is a prime breeding ground for problems. Be aware. Have a pest management program in place. Keep a close eye out for troubles. They can happen quickly. Oftentimes a lot of damage is done before you realize the problem. Again, keep up with spraying. Then be sure to keep records of what you sprayed and when. This is valuable information to have for both you and your inspector.

Feeding

All plants should be fed on a weekly basis. Water-soluble plant foods work best for bedding plants. I recommend using a 20-20-20 plant food one week and a high phosphate food the next. These two work out well. Plants will grow at an accelerated rate in a greenhouse, as you know. Fertilizer keeps them healthy and will produce more color.

Watering

This is a tricky one. You can over- or under-water quite easily in a greenhouse. Since all plants require different amounts of water, you'll have to keep a close watch on watering. Plants near fans or the heater tend to dry out faster than others may. Plants on the afternoon sun side will tend to need more water too. However, your greenhouse is a closed environment. Your transpiration rate (moisture loss) is much less. This being said, there's always a lot of moisture inside. Be careful with mostly over-, sometimes under-, watering.

Pinching

As plants grow at a quicker rate, they need to be spaced (as previously mentioned) and pinched back. Pinching creates more side branching and makes plants fuller, and ultimately nicer. Not all plants will require pinching. But again, you most likely know all this already. Just a friendly reminder. Compact plants with more branches will create more flower buds. This makes them marketable faster.

Weeds

As previously stated, weeds have no place in your greenhouse. It's best to spray them before you put anything inside the house. Don't let weeds go to seed or you'll have more problems. Weeds are a magnet for insects. You can greatly decrease a potential insect population by getting your greenhouse weed free first. Greenhouse production can be tricky enough without more to worry about. Sterile, weed-free conditions are best.

A Few Final Notes

✔ Watch for slick floors. This will be especially important for your customers. Algae and moss on the floor can be common. Eradicate the problem before it starts.

✔ Hot summer sun can be minimized with shade cloth. Shade cloth is available in various densities from thirty to eighty percent. You will have to determine what will be best for you. Shade cloth is available at numerous nursery supply companies.

✔ Keeping your plants' needs in mind, it's best to rotate your crops often. This helps with adequate sun exposure as needed within the greenhouse.

You and the Community

BECOMING A FAMILIAR NAME in your community takes time. You'll have to advertise and have word of mouth spread your garden center around. As previously mentioned in the Advertising chapter, you need to get, and keep, your name out there. There is really no such thing as spreading your name around town too much. In fact, the more people are familiar with your name the better. People that aren't your customers (yet) will feel like they're missing out if they don't visit your store! This is true. Some of the tried and true ways of getting known are:

- ✔ sponsoring a kids baseball team
- ✔ conducting free how-to seminars
- ✔ sponsoring a local gardening show
- ✔ free classes with local gardening experts
- ✔ clinics and classes on various subjects
- ✔ a display at your local fair
- ✔ having a float in your local parades
- ✔ having a booth at the home and garden show
- ✔ having a spring kickoff barbecue at your nursery
- ✔ doing a monthly garden column in one of your local free publications

Plaster your name everywhere you can. The more you're seen, the more attention you'll create. Exposure is the name of the game. Other ideas to get noticed are:

- ✔ your name on the work delivery van
- ✔ your name on the golf course benches
- ✔ your name on park benches,
- ✔ a banner on your local city buses
- ✔ anywhere else your name will be seen

Donations

Every event imaginable will seek you out for donations. You sell color; that's what they want. Others are looking for a piece of garden giftware to raffle off at their event. Donations are a good way to be recognized in your community. Some donating is good. However, be careful; it can get out of hand. Chances are good that if you donate to someone's cause, they'll be back next year. Chances are also good that the word will circulate between donation seekers. The question remains: Is donating going to get your business recognized? Maybe a small mention at their function. If so, that's good exposure. What it really comes down to is this: The person asking for the donation in the first place is most likely a customer of yours. For the small gesture the donation brings, you've actually helped your customer. You benefit from their return business.

Never Forget

- ✔ Your store, your money, your dream.
- ✔ You're only as strong as your weakest link.
- ✔ Quality, service, selection, and value every day.
- ✔ Study your balance sheet and profit and loss statement.
- ✔ Teach your crew.
- ✔ Know about everything you sell.
- ✔ Try to keep the money you make in the spring.
- ✔ Lead by example.
- ✔ Communication is key.
- ✔ Expect the unexpected.
- ✔ Build a strong image.
- ✔ Advertise.
- ✔ Get the money from the bank you need.
- ✔ Find your niche.
- ✔ Price everything.
- ✔ Think before you lift.
- ✔ Wear your smile.

- ✔ Be complete with watering.
- ✔ Keep your finger on the pulse.
- ✔ Use tie-in sales.
- ✔ Sell, sell, sell.
- ✔ Change is everything.
- ✔ Keep your inventory moving.
- ✔ Don't let the public set your pace.
- ✔ Plant trees straight in pots.
- ✔ There is no kink-free hose.

About the Author

Greg Moore has been in the retail garden center business since 1980. He possesses ornamental horticulture and business degrees. Greg has strong knowledge of how the business works. He has created five garden centers from the ground up. This includes several award-winning nurseries. He is the previous owner of Greg's Gardens and Gifts in Longview, Washington for twenty years. This is his seventh published work on plants. He lives with his wife in Chehalis, Washington.

Other Publications by Greg Moore

Greg's guide to growing fruits and vegetables
Greg's guide to growing perennials
Greg's guide to growing annuals
Greg's guide to common sense gardening
Greg's guide Frequently asked gardening Questions
The Day by Day gardening calendar

www.ingramcontent.com/pod-product-compliance
Lightning Source LLC
LaVergne TN
LVHW051646080426
835511LV00016B/2522